THE PRODIGAL SPIRIT:

The Trinity, the Church and the
Future of the World

THE PRODIGAL SPIRIT:

The Trinity, the Church and the
Future of the World

GRAHAM TOMLIN

ISBN: 978 1 905887 00 2

Scripture quotations taken from the
HOLY BIBLE, NEW INTERNATIONAL VERSION.
Copyright © 1973, 1978, 1984 by International Bible Society.
Used by permission of Hodder & Stoughton Publishers,
A member of the Hachette Livre UK Group.
All rights reserved.
"NIV" is a registered trademark of International Bible Society.
UK trademark number 1448790.

Prodigal Son image is a photograph of the
original sculpture by Charlie Mackesy

Published by Alpha International
Holy Trinity Brompton
Brompton Road
London SW7 1JA
Email: publications@alpha.org

A catalogue record for this book is available from
the British Library

Typeset in 10/12.5 Palatino
Printed and bound in Great Britain by MPG Books

CONTENTS

Graham Tomlin combines biblical depth, accessible theology and rich experience within one of the world's most dynamic churches – he also 'flies' imaginatively, intellectually and in his engagement with urgent personal and public issues. This wise book inspires, nurtures and stretches its readers.

David F. Ford, Regius Professor of Divinity, University of Cambridge

Simultaneously learned, imaginative, accessible, and long overdue. A coherent understanding of the Spirit as the one who draws us and the whole of creation into the knowledge of the love of God, which is the love between the Father and the Son, is applied to a range of key issues for the church and the world. This book will help its readers to break out of partial emphases on the work of the Spirit to embrace the whole.

Bishop Graham Cray, Archbishop's Missioner

Masterfully portraying the role and activity of the Spirit in contemporary society, The Prodigal Spirit *is a fresh and profound new theological perspective that offers hopeful insights to the church as it strives to be relevant in an increasingly complex world.*

Robert (Bob) Lupton, Founder FCS Urban Ministries, Atlanta, Georgia, USA

Graham Tomlin is one of the most gifted theological teachers and communicators in today's church. He has that rare gift of being able to express complex theological ideas in ways that are accessible and applicable, and so deepen our discipleship. The Prodigal Spirit *is a book of considerable spiritual discernment, counsel and vision.*

Revd. Canon Professor Martyn Percy, Principal, Ripon College, Cuddesdon

INTRODUCTION

Who are we and what are we here for? These are two of the most profound questions we can ever ask ourselves. Twenty-first century societies are littered with dislocated people who don't know who they are or what their purpose is in life. Greater mobility – both social and geographical – is a great thing, opening up possibilities and opportunities that our grandparents could hardly have dreamt of. However, it can often leave people rootless, constantly moving, never quite sure where they really belong. We do not lack today for labour-saving devices, or means of amusing ourselves to while away the hours, flicking over the Internet, watching another DVD on demand or grazing over endless channels of cable TV. Constant entertainment can be enjoyable up to a point, but can also lead to an unsettled restlessness, time frittered away on triviality, and a frustrating lack of purpose or direction.

Lacking a sense of identity and drifting from one day to the next without a clue about what they are doing on earth, many people struggle through life with at best a sense of listless anomie, at worst a lingering sense of depression. On the other hand, knowing your identity and vocation is a huge step towards living a contented and fulfilled life. A sure sense that you know who you are, where you are rooted and to whom you belong, as well as a strong sense of conviction that you are here for a reason, and know what that reason is, brings a stability and security that is enviable when you see it.

This book tries to address these questions of identity and

purpose through the lens of one central Christian idea: the theology of the Holy Spirit, or to give it its longer name, pneumatology.

This is a theology profoundly needed in the twenty-first century. Contemporary societies desperately need cohesion and a deep sense of common life and purpose. The fragmentation of the former eastern bloc in the 1990s, the religious conflicts that have shaken global confidence since the rise of militant Islam, the continued growth in the gap between rich and poor, all make us painfully aware of division and disharmony. The search is not just for a common set of values (probably impossible to find in an irreversibly pluralist society), but a deeper common spirit, a sense of kindness, peace, patience, gentleness towards one another. These of course are the classic Christian gifts of the Spirit. The Holy Spirit is for Christians the source of all community and cohesion. At almost every church service Christians invoke the 'fellowship of the Holy Spirit' along with the grace of our Lord Jesus Christ and the love of God. The New Testament emphasises the Spirit's work in drawing what would otherwise be dissonant chaos into varied unity. The unity of the Spirit is not uniformity but harmony in difference – precisely what a divided world and church needs.

Then there is the ecological crisis. David Attenborough recently said: 'I'm no longer sceptical. I don't have any doubt at all. I think climate change is the major challenge facing the world today.' One of the central themes in biblical pneumatology is that the Spirit 'broods over the creation' (Gn. 1.2) and 'renews the face of the earth.' (Ps. 104.30). The experience of the Spirit is a foretaste, deposit, or first fruits here and now of the new creation, the world that one day will come. The bold Christian claim is that the Holy Spirit is the hope for the future of the earth – that we are not alone in our attempts to save the planet. We are working with the Spirit of God who gives life and power to renew a damaged earth.

At the same time, the church, at least in western Europe, is also in dire need of a new start. Faced by scandals, moral and theological quarrels and numerical decline, if the church in this continent is to stand any chance of revival and renewal, it will need a fresh wave of the Spirit, yet one that breaks out of the narrow confines of the charismatic to infuse all traditions of the church. As Archbishop Rowan Williams recently said: 'It is the work of the Spirit that heals the Body of Christ, not the plans or the statements of any group, or any person, or any instrument of communion.' The church sorely needs a fresh breath of the Spirit who makes all things new.

Theology also needs the Spirit. We all know how theological study can become arid, divisive, and dull. Theology in the Spirit, as the Greek Fathers, for example, always envisaged it, is different. Rather than an object of theological enquiry, the Spirit makes engaged, worshipful theological enquiry possible, by bringing us into relationship with the God into whom we enquire with our minds. In other words, if we are to take the theology of the Spirit with full seriousness, it will engage us immediately in the realm of encounter – the intimate closeness of being brought into the life and love at the heart of God the Holy Trinity, not just in theory but in practice and experience – so that our theology gets imagined within that experience, not outside of it. A theology of the Spirit will be a matter of the heart as well as the mind.

The Prodigal Spirit

The title of this book may need some explanation. Most people know the story of the Prodigal Son. It is the story of a boy who goes out from his father's house to a far country. Having wasted his inheritance lavishly, recklessly, he returns, is embraced by his father and welcomed home. It might seem odd to speak of the prodigal Spirit, but as we shall see there are all kinds of resonances between this story and the theology of the Spirit. The Spirit too is sent out from the Father into the far country of a world that has turned its back on the divine Father. The Spirit is also lavish, although in a way that is generous, not reckless, in giving away the good things that he has from the Father's presence. He also returns to the embrace of love that flows from the Father's heart. A further level of the Spirit's connection to the story of the prodigal son and the father remains to be explored in the book itself, but that will do for the time being to establish a positive prodigality as a feature of the Spirit's work.

The Holy Spirit draws us and the whole of creation into the knowledge of the love of God, which is the love between the Father and the Son. The Spirit unites us with Christ, and so we can know for ourselves the love of the Father for the Son. Christian life, life in the Spirit, is therefore living in this love, living day by day in the realm of the love of God. When we start to live in this space, we find a new identity as those loved by the Father in Christ, and a new purpose: to prepare for the new creation, which Jesus initiated by his words and actions, and of which the Holy Spirit is a foretaste and anticipation. Only a full understanding and experience of the love of God in Christ through the Spirit can restore a proper sense of identity and vocation.

The book has benefited from the comments and reflections of many people with whom I have discussed it over the past few years. In particular, I am grateful to Pete Bellenger, Tom Weinandy, David Ford, Charles Foster, Mark Knight, Rob McDonald, James Orr, Ken Costa and Nicky Gumbel. My colleagues at St Paul's Theological Centre, Holy Trinity Brompton and St Mellitus College have also provided a wonderfully stimulating environment in which to do theology. I'm particularly grateful to Jane Williams (whose idea the title was), Michael Lloyd, David Hilborn, Andrew Emerton, Stephen Backhouse, Ann Coleman and Lincoln Harvey for their friendship, encouragement and for making theology and work such fun. Special thanks are due to Hector and Caroline Sants, in whose spacious and comfortable library much of this book was written. Their ever generous hospitality and friendship means a great deal to Janet and me.

Part of my work is closely related to a local church, Holy Trinity Brompton (HTB), with the energy and dynamic that comes from seeing a stream of people, many of them young, finding Christ and being touched by the Spirit through the Alpha course developed there. I have been conscious of the huge benefits of doing theology in a context intimately linked to the life of the church. It keeps theology honest by always asking questions about its coherence with the stories of those discovering and living life in the Spirit, and about its closeness and usefulness to the life of the church. This book has at least in part emerged from the experience of watching and being part of the Holy Spirit at work within HTB and the Alpha network around the world. It is not an official 'theology of Alpha', but rather some theological reflections that have emerged in the course of being involved in this remarkable church and ministry that has at the time of writing seen 15 million people take the course and over 50,000 churches run it, of all kinds of shapes, sizes and denominations. Perhaps today we need not just a theology *of* the Holy Spirit, but theology done *in* the Holy Spirit. Theology in the Spirit has to be theology done close to the community of the Spirit, the temple of God, the body of Christ in which the Spirit chooses to make Christ known. It has been a privilege to study, work, pray and minister in such a context and I thank God for it.

The prayer 'Come, Holy Spirit' is one of the oldest prayers of the church. It is also a prayer often prayed with expectation in HTB, in other similar churches and on Alpha courses around the world. This book is in some ways an explanation of what we might expect to happen when we pray that prayer with all seriousness. My prayer as you read this book is that the Spirit will indeed come to bring understanding where it gets things right, forgetfulness where it is mistaken, and the renewed sense of identity and purpose that comes from knowing the love of God that transforms us and all creation into what we were always meant to be.

CHAPTER 1

THE HOLY SPIRIT
AND IDENTITY

Who am I? There are few people who have not asked this
question at some point in their lives. Where did I come from,
where do I belong? How do I best describe myself? And then
there are questions of purpose – what am I here for? Is there
a purpose to life? All these are deep existential questions that
need an answer. This book is designed to help find an answer
to those questions, by looking more closely at the Christian
doctrine of the Holy Spirit, which might just hold some vital
clues to finding a way forward.

Towards the end of his life, the great Swiss theologian Karl
Barth, who had for most of his life focused his considerable
theological thought around the centrality of Christ, began
to dream of a theology which would be focused on the Holy
Spirit, a theology that he, like Moses, was only allowed to see
from afar. In this kind of theology, 'Everything which needs to
be said, considered and believed about God the Father and God
the Son ... might be shown and illuminated in its foundations
through God the Holy Spirit, the *vinculum pacis inter Patrem et
Filium*.'[1]

How might such a theology work? Or perhaps more
importantly, how might such a theology help us work out
questions of identity and vocation? How might it help the

---

1. Barth, K. (ed. D. Ritschl), *The Theology of Schleiermacher: Lectures at Göttingen, winter semester of
1923/24* (Edinburgh: T. & T. Clark, 1998), 277f.

church provide answers to these questions, and be renewed and re-imagined in the twenty-first century? At least in its traditional heartlands in the West (if not in the global South and East) the church is struggling to be heard or taken seriously any more. Perhaps a renewed focus on the theology of the Spirit and in the life of the Spirit might hold the key.

The Spirit in Christian Theology

The history of the church's understanding of the Trinity, and specifically its understanding of the role of the Spirit in the Trinity, has been the source of much theological hand-wringing over the centuries. Although pretty well agreed that God is best described as 'three-in-one', the church has struggled to understand and agree the precise relationship between the three persons in the Trinity. A chief bone of contention has been the dispute over the relationship between Father, Son and Spirit between Eastern and Western churches for over a millennium now, perhaps an indication in itself that the church as a whole is still struggling to understand Scripture aright on this vital question. Put simply, the Western Church (both Protestant and Catholic) has held that the Father begets the Son, and the Holy Spirit proceeds from the Father and the Son together (the famous *filioque* clause). The Eastern churches see this as denying the monarchy, or distinct originating role of the Father within the Trinity, by suggesting that the Spirit proceeds from the Son as well as the Father, whereas this is properly the sole work of the Father. They also accuse the West of diminishing the Holy Spirit by making him subordinate to the other two persons, and therefore of less importance. Meanwhile, some strands of modern theology call a plague on both houses, accusing both of being too concerned for abstract divine being, which seems irrelevant to both divine revelation and human life.

A common critique of the Western understanding of the Trinity is its implication that while the Father and Son are active in begetting and issuing, the Holy Spirit is the somewhat passive member of the Trinity, simply proceeding from the other two. To take one influential example, St Augustine of Hippo's idea of the Spirit as the bond of love between the Father and the Son[2] could imply that the two primary constituent parts of the Godhead are the Father and Son, and that the Spirit is simply the passive 'glue' that ties them together. Augustine seems to subsume the Spirit into the relationship between the Father and the Son, which leads to the question of whether the Spirit is anything different from the divine substance itself, or even whether the Spirit is less than personal – a bond and not a person.[3] Of course, Augustine is seeking to stress other aspects of the Trinitarian life, but his approach can be read as endorsing a view of the Trinity that leaves the Spirit as passive, impersonal and subordinate. Furthermore, Augustine's massively influential theology of grace, developed in controversy with the Pelagians, soon came to overshadow the notion of the Spirit, so that functions attributed to the Spirit (transformation, healing etc.) came to be attributed instead to divine *grace*, especially within the sacramental theology of the Middle Ages. As a result, within medieval theology, pneumatology was largely lost within the theology of grace, and does not play a prominent role in the theological discussion of that time.[4]

---

2. For example, '... his being suggests to us that mutual charity whereby the Father and Son love each other.' *De Trinitate* XV.27, or as Eberhard Jüngel puts it while discussing this point, 'In the Spirit, the Father and the Son affirm each other mutually.' Jüngel, E., *God as the Mystery of the World: On the Foundations of the Theology of the Crucified One in the Dispute between Theism and Atheism* (Edinburgh: T. & T. Clark, 1983), 388.
3. See Badcock, G. D., *Light of Truth and Fire of Love: A Theology of the Holy Spirit* (Grand Rapids: Eerdmans, 1997), 67–75.
4. For example, Aquinas' *Summa Theologica* treats the Holy Spirit under the general section entitled 'Father, Son and Holy Ghost' (Ia.33-43). In the *Tertia Pars*, there is a section on 'The Incarnate Word' and 'Our Lady', but none on the Holy Spirit. The theme of the Spirit is revisited in the section on virtues and the moral life later on in the *Summa*, yet it seems to be primarily located in the ethical rather than more strictly theological section of the work.

The Spirit and the Trinity in Eastern Theology

Eastern theology complains that the West has effectively downgraded the Spirit in comparison to the other persons of the Trinity due to this doctrine of the 'double procession'. It protests at what it sees as an undervaluing of the Spirit. Eastern dislike of the *filioque* is usually attributed to insistence on the monarchy of the Father – the Father as the sole originator of divinity. The East proposes, like the West, that the Father begets the Son, but maintains that the Spirit, like the Son, proceeds from the Father alone, to preserve the full divinity of the Spirit.

Western theologians have replied that this emphasis on the monarchy of the Father can imply that logically, if not ontologically, the Father is the only one who is truly divine, that all of the godhead resides in him alone, and therefore in a sense, he does not need the other two persons. It also implies that the other two persons are divine only by derivation not by nature. Moreover, it does not establish a clear relationship between the Spirit and the Son, opening the way for the idea that there can be an experience of the Spirit that is not connected in some way to the incarnate Word. Here, the Spirit is not *necessarily* the Spirit of Jesus. This leaves the Spirit as somewhat indeterminable – we cannot say what shape or form he comes in, or how he is to be recognised. Many observers suggest that in the east, this has sometimes led to the controlling of the Spirit by the institution of the church. If the Spirit is not necessarily the Spirit of Jesus, and therefore we do not really know what he is like, it is a short step from there to an all-controlling church that is all too ready to claim to dictate what the Spirit can and cannot do. Tying the Spirit closely to the historical Jesus prevents any individual or church from recreating the Spirit in their own image. It gives a criterion of external control to help evaluate claims that the Spirit is speaking through those particular individuals or churches. Anyone can claim that the Spirit is speaking through them. A vital test is whether that voice sounds like the voice of Jesus.

The Spirit and the Trinity in Protestant Theology

The sixteenth-century reformers did not by and large engage
in extensive exploration of new approaches to the Trinity.
Luther tied the Spirit closely to the word and the sacraments,
although it has to be said pneumatology was not the focus of
his theological work.[5] Calvin's theology of the Spirit is more
creative and interesting. For him, the heart of Christian faith is
union with Christ, which is brought about by the Spirit.[6] Faith
is the result, not the precondition of the work of the Spirit in a
person.[7] For Calvin, the Spirit enables us to access the work of
Christ, or in other words, the work of Christ is of no use to us
unless the Spirit unites us with him.[8] Yet Calvin's position can
imply, as later Calvinism certainly took him to mean, that the
Spirit only confirms the word, and thus is subservient to it or
unable to work in any other way than through the word.

This Protestant tendency to tie the Spirit to the word might
be less problematic in terms of Trinitarian theology if the 'Word'
is taken to mean the divine 'Logos', incarnate in Jesus the Son.
However, given the Protestant tendency to use 'word' to refer
primarily to the Bible, it can lead to the Spirit being enclosed
within the word of Scripture or preaching alone, and unable to
speak or act apart from the read or preached word of the Bible.
Following Luther and Calvin, Protestant theology has often
been concerned to avoid the close link between the Spirit and
the magisterium of the church that led to an unaccountable
medieval church, claiming authority for what sometimes
seemed to be novel doctrines and abuses of power. Its answer
was to tie the Spirit not so much to the teaching office of the
church or to tradition, but to the word of Scripture, to free the
church from the 'tyranny' of human control of the Spirit, yet the

---

5. Though see Prenter, R., *Spiritus Creator: Luther's Concept of the Holy Spirit* (Philadelphia: Fortress,
1953), who shows that while Luther tied the Spirit closely to the Word and the Sacrament, he does
recognise a 'hiatus' between them. We cannot assume the Spirit's presence in Word and Sacrament
as the medieval Catholic church did, but have to pray for it and long for it.
6. Calvin, J., *Institutes of the Christian Religion* (London: Collins, 1986), III.1.1: 'the Holy Spirit is the
bond by which Christ effectually unites us to himself.'
7. *Ibid.*, III.1.4: 'faith is the principal work of the Holy Spirit.'
8. *Ibid.*, III.1.1: 'as long as Christ remains outside of us, and we are separated from him, all that he
has suffered and done for the salvation of the human race remains useless and of no value for us.'

result was often that the Spirit's voice was heard only through Scripture and its exposition, and his presence only recognised when that word was expounded by an official preacher.

This Protestant tendency has sometimes led to a virtual identity of the Scripture and the Spirit, so that it becomes hard to distinguish conceptually or even experientially between them. The Spirit then has no independent life apart from the Word, and it is a short step from there to tying the Spirit to the word of the preacher – arguably a form of human captivity of the Spirit every bit as problematic as being tied to the organs of the church's official papal teaching. It implies taking the Scriptures as the sole *source* of truth rather than the *instrument* of the Spirit of truth, suggesting that the Bible is the only place where truth is found, rather than the place we go to evaluate and discern truth found elsewhere in God's world. When the Spirit is bound this closely to the word, there is little sense left of a genuine freedom of the Spirit.

As mentioned above, another strand of Protestant theology has tended to emphasise the close relationship between Word and Spirit in a different sense – that is, using 'Word' not so much for the Bible, but for the 'Word made flesh', the incarnate Son of God. Karl Barth's theology is an example of this Protestant inclination to focus God's revelation christologically, to the exclusion of any form of divine revelation that does not come through Christ. This of course bars the way to any natural, direct knowledge of God in creation, yet it also means that Barth has little place for specific revelation through the Holy Spirit. The Spirit becomes tied to Christ in that he is solely the Spirit of Christ. This naturally is a vital point. Scarred by his experience during two twentieth-century world wars, Barth was keen to avoid any sense that the Spirit spoke apart from Christ, for example through historical events and whoever happened to be in political power at any moment, such as the National Socialists. Hence he insisted, especially in his earlier theology, on tying the Spirit closely to Christ and as a result mounted a vigorous defence of the *filioque* clause, with its close association of the Spirit with Christ. However, he does this in such a way that seems to deny any distinct role for the Spirit. For Barth, the Spirit's role is primarily retrospective, reminding us of Christ and making Christ real to us. He has little place for what we will see in due course of the vital biblical and eschatological work of the Spirit in being a foretaste of the age to come.[9]

The Spirit and the Trinity in Modern Theology

More recent Christian thinking offers a critique of much previous Trinitarian thought, judging many traditional formulations to be too abstract and unconnected to human life and divine revelation. The Roman Catholic theologian Karl Rahner's famous dictum that 'the 'economic' Trinity is the 'immanent' Trinity and the 'immanent' Trinity is the 'economic' Trinity' forms exactly such a critique.[10] In other words, this means that God as he is revealed to us is the same as God as he is in himself. There is no hidden aspect of God separate from revelation, no secret inner being upon which we are encouraged to speculate. For Rahner, the benefit of this approach is to present the Trinity as a doctrine that has to do with salvation, and therefore with humanity, rather than God in glorious or not-so-glorious isolation. One influential way in which this has been developed is the move towards what is called the 'social Trinity', arguing that the Trinity is primarily about relationship and interaction rather than divine substance and identity.[11] In this approach, the doctrine of the Trinity tells us that God is relational in his very being – at the heart of God there is relationship and community, rather than isolation or hierarchy. Both of these approaches emphasise the extent to which God's nature is bound up in his relationships with his creation, or at least they suggest that it is of little use for us to speculate on

9. Rosato, P. J., *The Spirit as Lord: the Pneumatology of Karl Barth* (Edinburgh: T. & T. Clark, 1981), although see also Thompson, J., *The Holy Spirit in the Theology of Karl Barth* (Allison Park: Pickwick Publications, 1991), who seeks to defend Barth against these charges.
10. Rahner, K., *The Trinity* (London: Burns and Oates, 1970), 22.
11. See for example Moltmann, J., *The Trinity and the Kingdom of God* (London: SCM, 1981).

God's inner being (the immanent Trinity). Rather, we only really have an interest in how God relates to us.

This approach is not without its critics.[12] Some versions of the 'social Trinity' can lean towards a form of tri-theism that the Fathers studiously avoided. Despite assurances to the contrary, making interrelationality the essence of God conjures up the idea of three separate persons, or individual beings in relationship with one another.[13] As Norman Metzler puts it:

> ... that the mutual self-differentiation in the Godhead, which the fathers did assert, implies three independent, personal centres of action in eternal relationship with one another as in some sense plural entities, would seem to extend decisively beyond the bounds of the intent of the Trinitarian doctrine, and invite us to embrace some type of personalistic tritheism.[14]

In particular this notion of the social Trinity is difficult to figure out in relation to the Holy Spirit. According to classic Christian formulations of the doctrine, the Spirit is a distinct 'person' within the Trinity, yet he is clearly a person in a different sense from the Father and the Son, whose very names imply interrelationality and personhood. For example, while the New Testament contains many assurances that the Father loves the Son, and the Son loves the Father, we never read that the Father or the Son loves the Spirit or vice versa. It is not that they are indifferent towards the Spirit, nor the Spirit indifferent towards them, but that is just not the best way to describe the relationship. The relationship between the Father and the Son is different from the relationships between the Father and the Spirit, and the Son and the Spirit. Within many descriptions of the social Trinity, it is hard to see how the Spirit plays a distinct

12. See for example Gresham, J., 'The Social Model of the Trinity and its Critics', *Scottish Journal of Theology* 46 (1993); Kilby, K., 'Perichoresis and Projection: Problems with the Social Doctrines of the Trinity', New Blackfriars (2000); Metzler, N. (2003), 'The Trinity in Contemporary Theology: Questioning the Social Trinity' *Concordia Theological Quarterly* 67: 270–87.
13. A version of this in more popular writing is the widely read novel *The Shack*, in which the three persons of the Trinity are depicted as three individual people living together in a shack in the woods. Young, W. P., *The Shack* (London: Hodder, 2008).
14. Metzler, 'The Trinity in Contemporary Theology'.

role within the Godhead, since 'Spirit' is not a personal category in the same way as 'Father' and 'Son' are. This approach can tend to blur the distinctive role of the Spirit by making him play the same role of interrelationality as the two other persons of the Godhead.

To sum up this brief glance at the main contours of historical pneumatology, it can be argued that in their turn, Catholic, Orthodox, Protestant and modern theologies each stress something vital about the Trinity and the Spirit, yet they are all incomplete on their own. Western theology emphasises the vital link between the Son and the Spirit, yet tends to subordinate the Spirit to the Son, implying the Spirit is less divine than the other two persons. This has sometimes led to a collapsing of the Spirit into an authoritarian church (in the Catholic version of the story) and into authoritarian teachers of the Bible (in the Protestant version), and thus has restricted the freedom of the Spirit. Eastern theology, on the other hand, helpfully emphasises the primacy of the Father, yet fails to establish a clear relationship between the Son and the Spirit, leaving the Spirit floating free from God's revelation in Jesus, opening the door to the 'Christless mysticism' that Karl Barth thought he saw in Eastern orthodoxy.[15] Modern conceptions valuably emphasise the importance of relationship and community at the heart of God, yet perhaps lose something of the essential oneness of God and the distinct role of the Spirit within the Trinity.

Each of these approaches has struggled to find the right space for the Holy Spirit. One recent account of the theology of the Holy Spirit concludes: 'the claim of contemporary Trinitarian theology to a more adequate pneumatological position than the older tradition can be exaggerated. The doctrine of the Trinity today remains a crucial area of theological controversy, and pneumatology is in many ways one of its weakest links.'[16] Perhaps a symptom or sign of this is the fact that often such discourse feels like a rather arid

---

15. See Tom Smail's essay on 'The Holy Spirit and the Trinity' in Seitz, C. (ed.), *Nicene Christianity: the Future for a New Ecumenism* (Grand Rapids, MI: Brazos Press, 2001).
16. Badcock, *Light of Truth and Fire of Love*, 212.

discussion of the Trinity as an object of study and analysis. The early Christian Fathers on the other hand were keen to insist that theology is not an abstract science but an engaged search. *Theologia* in the East in particular is really a form of prayer and contemplation before it is an academic subject. As Evagrius Ponticus, the fourth-century monastic theologian put it: 'If you are a theologian, you will pray truly. And if you pray truly, you are a theologian.'[17] Is there a way of more adequately articulating the status of the Spirit and his relation to the other persons of the Trinity, and in the process, discovering what Karl Barth was searching for in a more thoroughgoing pneumatological theology?

The Father's Spirit of Sonship

In a brief but stimulating and creative book, Tom Weinandy suggests that these problems are due (especially in the East) to the residue of 'neo-Platonic emanationist sequentiality' in Patristic doctrines of the Trinity.[18] In other (and simpler) words, the early Fathers, in developing and expounding the doctrine could not help formulating it in language borrowed from Platonic understandings of God that assumed 'grades' of divinity. Beings could be divine, or semi-divine, and 'lesser' divine beings emanated from 'more' divine beings (this notion for example enabled the development of apotheosised Roman emperors being seen as divine and therefore to be worshipped in later pagan practice). Thus in both the Latin west and the Greek east, this led to the subtle implication that there was hierarchy and subordination built into the Trinity, that the three persons were not all divine to the same extent.

Weinandy argues that the problem in both parts of the Christian world has been an inadequate doctrine of the Holy Spirit. Emerging from his own experience[19] of being filled with

17. Evagrius Ponticus, *On Prayer*, §61.
18. Weinandy, T., *The Father's Spirit of Sonship: Reconceiving the Trinity* (Edinburgh: T. & T. Clark, 1995).
19. *Ibid.*, x.

the Holy Spirit in the Roman Catholic context, his proposal is that 'the Son is begotten by the Father in the Spirit and thus the Spirit simultaneously proceeds from the Father as the one in whom the Son is begotten.'[20] The Spirit is the 'fatherly love' in which the Son is begotten. This might sound complex and unnecessarily intricate, but the implications are important. This way of describing the Trinity preserves an active and vital role for the Spirit in the begetting of the Son, rather than this happening without him. It reflects the stories in the gospels, such as the infancy narratives, in which Jesus is conceived by or through the Holy Spirit, and the accounts of Jesus' baptism, which give a central role to the Spirit in the designation of Jesus as God's Son. John's Gospel, where Jesus promises to send the Spirit on the disciples, suggests the *filioque* was right – the Father sends the Spirit through the Son.[21] However, the nativity and baptism stories seem to suggest that the Father sends the Son through the Spirit.[22] More immediately, this approach indicates how Christians are related to God in an analogous way – adopted as sons and daughters in and by the Holy Spirit. And this experience is itself an experience of life within the Trinity. As Weinandy puts it: 'through Baptism in the Spirit, our life within the Trinity moves from the realm of theological doctrine to that of lived experience.'[23] Christians are made sons and daughters of God in the same way as Christ was (though by adoption, not by nature) – through the gift of the Holy Spirit.

The Prodigal Spirit

This approach helpfully identifies the Spirit as the one who draws us into the experience of sonship of the Father and therefore into the love between the Father and Son. This can begin to help us understand a new approach to the Trinity.

20. *Ibid.*, 17.
21. See also for example Tit. 3.5–6: 'He saved us through the washing of rebirth and renewal by the Holy Spirit, whom he poured out on us generously through Jesus Christ our Saviour.'
22. See also for example Heb. 9.14, which speaks of 'Christ, who through the eternal Spirit offered himself unblemished to God.'
23. Weinandy, T., *The Father's Spirit of Sonship: Reconceiving the Trinity*, 106.

Charlie Mackesy is a Christian artist and sculptor, much of whose work explores the nature of the Christian faith. He is fascinated by the story of the Prodigal Son, and has produced a series of paintings, drawings and sculptures on this theme. Depicted here is the moment in Jesus' parable where the father embraces the prodigal son returning from his years in the wasteland of a misspent youth. It is a deeply evocative image, and captures a scene of deep emotion. The deep-set, yearning eyes and wide embrace of the father, and the helplessness and surrender of the son, capture the moment of reconciliation

brilliantly. The image works at two levels – one as a depiction
of this scene in Jesus' parable, and another as a picture of God's
welcome to the lost and weary soul coming back to him after a
lifetime away. Many people who have come to faith in Christ
over the years have found this image captures exactly what
they experienced when they came to Christian faith – the warm
embrace of the Father welcoming back a wayward child. Yet
there is perhaps a third level of interpretation of the image (and
by extension therefore the parable from which it derives). The
image can be seen as a window into the Trinity.

Karl Barth offered a Christological reading of the parable,
suggesting the idea that the Son of God follows the wayward
son (humanity) into 'the far country of a lost human existence'.
While warning against any over-simplistic equation of Jesus
Christ with the lost son of the parable, even still, 'in the going
out and coming in of the lost son in his relationship with the
father, we have a most illuminating parallel to the way trodden
by Jesus Christ in the work of atonement, to his humiliation
and exaltation.'[24] The journey of the son into the far country is
echoed by the journey of the Son of God, from the Father into a
lost and broken world, to take its pain and shame upon himself
all the way to a cross, only then to be raised and brought back
to the right hand of the Father.

If we let our imagination run with this way of looking at the
sculpture, it depicts God the Father embracing God the Son.
In particular it suggests the Father's embrace of the Son who
is on the borderline between life and death. In this sense, the
sculpture is a kind of *Pietà*, though not with Mary his mother
cradling the dead Jesus in her arms, but the Father embracing
the Son after his sacrifice on the cross. Bringing back the picture
to its setting in the Prodigal Son story, the words of the Father:
'for this son of mine was dead and is alive again' (Lk. 15.24)
makes the further connection with the resurrection. The image
captures the embrace in which the Father catches up and brings
to life the son who was dead and is alive again.[25]

24. Barth, K., *Church Dogmatics*, 4.2 §64.
25. The New Testament often implies that it was the Father who raised Jesus from death, for
example Acts 5.30; Rom. 4.24, 8.11.

Now of course there are only two persons in the picture – the Father and the Son, which leaves the question: where is the Holy Spirit? There is no visible depiction of the Spirit in the sculpture, but the way in which the image affects the observer hints at the role of the Spirit within it. That second level, the way in which many people have found themselves drawn into the image and begin to identify with the son, held and embraced by the father, is a sign of the place and work of the Spirit. If it were just a picture of a father and son embracing, it would simply be an interesting portrait of what might even be a self-enclosed exclusive love. Yet it is not. We are invited, welcomed into the picture – even into the very embrace between the Father and the Son, so that we begin to experience that same loving welcome, the same life-giving embrace of the Father for the Son. The Spirit is this invisible dimension of the sculpture – the invitation to become part of the embrace, to know and experience the love that pulses between the Son and the Father.

Irenaeus spoke of the Son and the Spirit as the 'two hands of God' and of how the Father does his work in the world through both the Son and the Spirit. It is a crucial reminder to us never to separate christology from pneumatology. It also suggests that if we can speak of Jesus Christ as the 'prodigal son' in the story, perhaps we should also imagine the Spirit as the 'prodigal Spirit'. Just as the Son of God is sent from the side of the Father into the far country of a rebellious and hurting world, so the Spirit is sent from the heart of God into that same far country to draw creation back into the embrace of the Father and the Son. There is, however, a sequence to this. In the gospels, the Spirit is sent upon the disciples only after the Son has offered his life as atonement, risen again and ascended to the Father. Once the Son has been reconciled to the Father, the Spirit is sent into the world to draw it back into the heart of God, which is the embrace between the Father and the Son. Pentecost follows after Good Friday, Easter and Ascension. The Spirit can only be sent after the restoration of the Son to the right hand of the

Father (Jn. 16.6). This is because the Spirit is related intimately to both Father and Son, and proceeds from the Father through the Son, from the very heart of the relationship between them, when the Son has returned to the intimacy of the Father's right hand. In the terms of the Prodigal Son picture, the Spirit is sent to draw us into the embrace between the Father and the Son.

Biblical Reflections

Two passages from the New Testament help to fill out this picture. The first is one of the great Trinitarian moments of the gospels: the baptism of Jesus. In this event, as the Holy Spirit descends on Jesus the Son, he hears the voice of the Father pronounced over him. As the Spirit comes on Jesus, the words spoken by the Father are hugely significant, as they offer the Father's ultimate 'verdict' on him, the full expression of the deepest core of the Father's heart turned towards the Son. They reveal the true identity of Jesus. The words are, of course: 'You are my Son, whom I love; with you I am well pleased' (Lk. 3.22). That is who Jesus essentially is: the beloved Son of the Father. He is not just the Son, he is the *beloved* Son. We all know children who are the genetic offspring of their parents, but who are not loved by those parents. Sonship does not necessarily mean love; however, here, in the divine relationship between the Father and the Son, it does. This describes the bond between the Father and the Son essentially as one of love. Not disapproval, ambivalence or disappointment, but love. The Son stands in the love of the Father, and this is the secret of his identity. In John's version of the baptism story, placed early on after the famous prologue, the Spirit comes down 'as a dove' upon Jesus. Although there is no voice from heaven at that point, the rest of John's Gospel can be seen as an exploration of the very theme of the love of the Father for the Son. In particular, John emphasises the way in which the love of the Father for the Son means a deep trust of the Son. Because he loves him, the Father entrusts him with all things (Jn. 3.35), entrusting all judgement to him (Jn. 5.20–22). If the figure of Jesus in the gospels breathes a deep sense of security and peace, it comes from his sure knowledge of the Father's love and trust.

The second passage is Romans 8. Here Paul develops this idea of our being brought by the Spirit into relationship with the Father:

> ... you received the Spirit of sonship. And by him we cry, 'Abba, Father.' The Spirit himself testifies with our spirit that we are God's children. Now if we are children, then we are heirs –heirs of God and co-heirs with Christ, if indeed we share in his sufferings in order that we may also share in his glory.

> **Romans 8.15–17**

Here, the Holy Spirit draws us into the same relationship that the Son has with the Father, so that we find ourselves using the same language as Jesus did – the intimate Aramaic term 'Abba'. We become children, heirs, standing in the same place in relation to the Father as Jesus does. More precisely, our relationship to the Father is defined by Jesus' relationship with the Father – we are his children only by being in Christ. Our sonship is not in any way parallel or separate from that of Jesus – it is only by virtue of being 'in Christ' that we become sons and daughters of God the Father. Of course, this relationship is established by grace rather than by nature, as a gift, rather than because we share the same essence as the Father. We are sons and daughters by adoption rather than by natural childbirth.[26] However, the language is still bold: we are drawn into the relationship between God the Father and God the Son (we will explore the significance of the reference to suffering here in the next chapter). It is only insofar as we are 'in Christ' that we know the full extent of the love of the Father (v. 39). Paul describes Christian initiation as being 'united with Christ' (Rom. 6.5), and Christian life repeatedly as being 'in Christ'.

---

26. Rom. 8.15; Gal. 4.5; Eph. 1.5.

When we place this next to the baptism story, which pinpoints love and trust as the central characteristics of the relationship between the Father and the Son, we begin to see more clearly the work of the Spirit in relationship to the Father and the Son.

The Spirit is not just conceived as the bond of love between the Father and the Son, as Augustine put it: his role is to draw us into that love by uniting us with the Son. As Calvin saw clearly: 'the Holy Spirit is the bond by which Christ effectually unites us to himself … he unites himself to us by the Spirit alone.'[27] The knowledge of the love of God for his Son becomes ours through the Holy Spirit. In Weinandy's terms, we become sons and daughters of the Father in the Spirit. The Spirit unites us with Christ, so that the love the Father has for him becomes the love he has for us – we are caught up into the love between the Father and the Son. Because we are in Christ through the Holy Spirit, we experience the same love of the Father as Jesus himself knows. Those who are in Christ are loved as Jesus is.

This leads to a number of important insights into Trinitarian theology. We are used to the simple New Testament saying 'God is Love' (1 Jn. 4.16). Yet these insights begin to give some shape and focus to this love. They tell us that at the heart of the universe pulses the love between the Father and the Son – this is the very essence of reality, the ultimate centre of all things. The love that appears here is not erotic, friendly or brotherly love – it is parental love. This is perhaps because in human experience, parental love is love at its most pure: it is a love between two people who share something deeper than a common sense of humour, interests or mutual attraction. They are bound together by something so profound that it cannot be dissolved by any decision to part. The relationship can be strained but it cannot be dissolved. The love of a parent for a child is also the only love we experience that is not motivated by something in the beloved. A mother loves her newborn child not because he can do anything for her, nor because of any beauty he possesses, but solely because he is her child. This is

---

27. Calvin, *Institutes*, III.1; III.3.

the nature of the love at the heart of God – the love between the Father and the Son.

This also brings us to the distinct role of the Spirit in the Trinity. This is not a possessive love that excludes others – it is an inclusive love that welcomes us to share in it. The Spirit is one of the 'persons' of the Trinity, yet he is a person in a different sense from the other two, because his role is different from theirs. The nature of the divine love is to create recipients of that love, to bring them into being and to enable them to reach their potential and fullness. The Spirit reaches out from the very centre of the love between the Father and Son, to enable us to find the healing and maturity that comes from living within the love of God. The Spirit is sent out from the heart of the bond between Father and Son, to draw creation back into that love as we will see more fully in the next chapter. Though the story focuses on the prodigal son, perhaps it is here that we might speak of the prodigal Spirit. One aspect of 'prodigality' is its lavishness, its unstinting generosity, its overflowing, almost reckless generosity. It describes the son in the far country giving away his inheritance with thoughtless abandon. Following Karl Barth's theological reading of the parable, perhaps it also describes the lavish generosity of the Spirit who reaches out from the heart of God to draw undeserving people back into an experience of that love.

The Creator Spirit

As the Spirit does this work of welcoming us into the love of God, we find a new identity. We become new people. People who come to faith in Christ often describe it as an experience of a new love for God and for people – it is as if they have been born all over again, which of course echoes the image Jesus himself uses in John's Gospel. Of course, we normally think of the Father as the primary 'Creator' in the Trinity, yet classic Christian theology insists that in every divine action all three persons of the Trinity are involved. In creation, the Spirit is involved every bit as much as the Father and the Son. In the great Christian hymn, *Veni Creator Spiritus*, probably composed by Rabanus Maurus, Abbot of Fulda in the ninth century, the Holy Spirit is boldly addressed as Creator. In human terms, the theme of the *Creator Spiritus* focuses on the theme of the creation of a new heart. As Psalm 51.10–11 has it:

> Create in me a pure heart, O God,
> and renew a steadfast spirit in me.
> Do not cast me from your presence
> or take your Holy Spirit from me.

The Spirit creates something new in human nature, a new and pure 'heart' that completes the human creation, making it fully capable of realising its potential in relation to God. The central petition of *Veni Creator Spiritus* says:

> Kindle a light in our senses
> Pour love into our hearts
> Infirmities of this body of ours
> overcoming with strength secure

This is a prayer for the creation of something new within us – a new light that brings to spiritual life the body that already has physical vigour, but lacks aliveness and alertness to God its Creator. The hymn goes on to specify what this 'new creation' consists of, in the penultimate verse:

> Grant we may know the Father through you
> And come to know the Son as well
> And may we always cling in faith
> To you, the Spirit of them both

When we speak of the Spirit creating a new heart within us, we mean the creation of a new appreciation of the Father and the

Son and beginning to participate in the love between them.[28] The Spirit beckons us to share in the love that the Father has for the Son, and the Son has for the Father. He is the prodigal Spirit of hospitality and welcome. As we come not just to understand that love, but to experience it and participate in it, we come to the fullness of what it really means to be created by the Father through the Son in the Spirit. It involves not just a physical existence, but something more: a spiritual awakening to love. This can be described as a new creation.[29] Now, in an important sense there is a genuine continuity with the old. Our past is not blanked out so that a completely new person emerges. However, we now realise who we really are. We are beloved sons and daughters of the Father, just as Jesus was, by virtue of being united with Christ by the Spirit. The Spirit is the one who brings us into relationship with the Father and the Son.

That last sentence is important and has to be stressed in a number of ways. On the one hand, it tells us that the Spirit does not exist for his own sake – his work with regard to humanity is to draw us into the embrace between the Father and the Son. On the other hand it needs to be read with the emphasis that it is the *Spirit* who brings us into relationship with the Father and the Son, and that needs to be said and taken with all due seriousness, rather than with a merely formal acknowledgement. People become beloved sons and daughters of God not through an intellectual discovery, moral improvement or liturgical practice, but through an encounter with the God who is love, through the Holy Spirit. Naturally this encounter may take place *through* intellectual enquiry, moral action or an act of worship, yet it is important to emphasise the theological priority of the work of the Spirit here. The Spirit alone makes Christians. It is the Spirit who brings about Christian life, worship and transformation. Is it through the Spirit that we are made sons and daughters of God.

---

28. This is a theme developed particularly by Fiddes, P. S., *Participating in God: A Pastoral Doctrine of the Trinity* (London: Darton, Longman & Todd, 2000). For him, it is not enough just to take the Trinity as a model for human community – the Trinity is itself an invitation to participate in the life of God.
29. 2 Cor. 5.17; Gal. 6.15.

This is an insight that the best theologians of the church have grasped clearly. Basil the Great writes: 'It is impossible to worship the Son, save by the Holy Spirit; impossible to call upon the Father, save by the Spirit of adoption.'[30] Again, 'If you remain outside the Spirit, you will not be able to worship at all.'[31] This is not just a focus of Patristic theology: John Calvin also insists that the Holy Spirit is the bond that unites us with Christ in whom are found all the treasures and goodness of God: 'Until our minds become intent upon the Spirit, Christ … lies idle because we coldly contemplate him as outside ourselves.'[32] It is an insight that finds a home at the heart of recent liberation theology as well. José Comblin, the Belgian Jesuit liberation theologian, writes: 'Once again we are discovering that the way we approach God, according to the Bible and true Christian tradition, is not through discursive reason, or our experience of creation, or through meditating on our inner being, but through a living experience of the Holy Spirit and its gifts. Only a spiritual experience, one of the Holy Spirit active in the community, can lead to the true God – the God of Jesus Christ, not a God of the philosophers.'[33]

The Spirit is God drawing us into God. Just as classical Christian theology has asserted that Jesus is the only way to the Father, in a similar way, the Spirit is the only way into experiencing the love that lies at the heart of God, the love of the Father for the Son, and to the transformation such knowledge brings. The Spirit is our 'way in' to God. The only way in which a person can be brought into a transforming experience of the love of God is through an encounter with the Holy Spirit.

Augustine characteristically insists on this point. The path to human transformation lies not through an act of the human will, or an intellectual activity, but through a work of the Holy Spirit. He describes what happens to a person in this process:

30. St Basil, *On the Holy Spirit* (Crestwood, New York: St Vladimir's Seminary Press, 1980), Ch. 11.
31. *Ibid.*, Ch. 9.
32. Calvin, *Institutes*, III.1 in McNeill, J. T., (ed.) and Battles, F.L. (trans.) *Calvin: Institutes of the Christian Religion* (Philadelphia: Westminster, 1961), 541.
33. Comblin, J., *The Holy Spirit and Liberation* (Maryknoll, New York: Burns and Oates, 1989), xi.

… he receives the Holy Spirit, whereby there arises in his soul
the delight in and the love of God, the supreme and changeless
Good. This gift is his here and now, while he walks by faith, not
yet by sight: that having this as earnest of God's free bounty, he
may be fired in heart to cleave to his Creator, kindled in mind to
come within the shining of the true light; and thus receive from
the source of his being the only true well-being.[34]

For him, as for the great tradition of Christian theology, the
Spirit is the one who enables us to respond to God. Without
the Spirit we are 'dead in [our] transgression and sins' (Eph.
2.1). The Spirit is the giver of life: he alone can bring a person to
life in the Spirit so that she becomes capable of responding to
God in worship, prayer and love. This is not just a point about
personality or preference, as if some Christians approach God
through the Spirit, some through the Father and some the Son
– it is a point with much greater theological depth. There is no
other way to know the love of the Father for the Son, the love
that lies at the heart of God, the love that lies at the very centre
of the universe, that alone can change and transform human
hearts, affections and behaviour, than through the Holy Spirit.

This is not to over-emphasise the Holy Spirit. It is to
consider properly the role of the Spirit in creation and new
creation, and to establish the right relations between the three
persons of the Trinity and the way in which human persons can
come to know God, and find out who they are. Knowledge of
God in the fullest sense of the word involves all three persons
of the Trinity, and a restoration of the active role of the Spirit
both within the Trinity itself and within our coming to a
knowledge of God serves only to restore biblical and historical
perspectives.

---

34. Augustine, *The Spirit and the Letter 5*, in Burnaby, J. (ed.) *Augustine: Later Works* (Library of
Christian Classics, Philadelphia: Westminster, 1955), 197.

Conclusion

This approach to the Trinitarian relations preserves the monarchy of the Father, as the one who loves and embraces the Son, and who sends the Spirit upon him to confirm him as Son (a point made very clear, as we have seen, in the stories of the baptism of Jesus in the gospels). At the same time, it establishes a clear link between the Spirit and the Son, in that as the Spirit of Christ, he draws us into union with Christ. It maintains an active and distinct role for the Spirit, yet one that is intimately related to the Father and the Son. It leads us directly into the heart of God – a heart of deep, passionate and compassionate love, a love that invites, welcomes and transforms.

It also offers a new vision of the theological task. If the Spirit is our 'way in' to the love of the Father and the Son, it tells us that God cannot be examined, studied or thought about adequately outside of that embrace of love, that proper knowledge (in the fullest sense of the word) of being enfolded in the love of God for his creation, which comes through the Spirit. Theology done outside of that knowledge will always ultimately fail to grasp who God is and what he means – it will lead to arid definitions and empty language. It is not so much a theology *of* the Spirit that we need as theology *in* the Spirit. When we take seriously the insight that our only access to the reality of God is through the Spirit, then we can develop a truly spiritual theology – theology which becomes not just an academic subject but an effective enquiry into the nature and work of God in the world, as personally engaged as it is intellectually rigorous.

Finally, it gives us a profound answer to the question with which we began: the question of human identity. Who are we? Christians can answer that question with a full Trinitarian confidence: because the Spirit has united us with Christ, we are beloved children of the Father, knowing the same love from the Father that Jesus knew. 'If anyone is in Christ', wrote St Paul, 'he is a new creation' (2 Cor. 5.17). We are a new creation, born again by the very same Spirit who brooded over the original creation. That gives a sure and confident identity that can both root and rebuild us. Whatever other identities we may have – whether national, ethnic, familial or professional – at a deeper level still, this is who we are: beloved children of the Father in Christ by the Spirit.

CHAPTER 2

THE HOLY SPIRIT AND CALLING

In his *Pensées*, Blaise Pascal wrote:

> When I consider the brief span of my life, absorbed into the eternity which comes before and after – *as the remembrance of a guest that tarrieth but a day* – the small space that I occupy and which I see swallowed up in the infinite immensity of spaces of which I know nothing and which knows nothing of me, I take fright and am amazed to see myself here rather than there: there is no reason for me to be here rather than there, now rather than then. Who put me here? By whose command and act were this time and place allotted to me?[1]

Pascal's questions are universal. Is there a reason why we are here? What is the purpose of the brief life we are given to live on earth? Does it have a purpose? Alongside the question of human identity, the question of human calling is perhaps the most urgent of our time or any time. The last chapter explored how the doctrine of the Trinity, explored through the lens of the Holy Spirit, helps us answer the question of human identity. Can the same approach help us answer the question of human vocation?

---

1. Pascal, B., *Pensées* (Harmondsworth: Penguin, 1966), L68, 48.

Creation and Christology

As we saw in the last chapter, the love of God is primarily the
love of the Father for the Son and vice versa. God's love is not
indiscriminate or unfocused, but is concentrated in his love for
the Son, the one worthy object of that love, and the one who
returns that love perfectly. All other aspects of the love of God
must therefore be related to this prior love. God loves in and
through the Son. Yet isn't that overly anthropocentric? Doesn't
it concentrate unhelpfully on humanity, feed the destructive
idea that human beings are all that matters about this world,
and therefore imply that the planet we inhabit is to be exploited
and mined simply for human use and pleasure? What then of
the rest of creation?

God's love precedes creation.[2] In fact you might say that
the creation emerges out of the love of God. It is in a sense
a product of the love we have already identified as the love
between the Father and the Son, which existed before creation
came into being. In the New Testament, there is a clear
relationship between creation and Christology. Creation takes
place in and through the Son – 'in him all things on heaven
and earth were created' (Col. 1.16, NRSV), and 'through him
all things were made' (Jn. 1.3). It therefore becomes the object
of God's love, because it was created 'in Christ'. Creation is
included in the love of God, because it came into being 'in him'.

In other words, it is not just us humans who are included in
the embrace of the Father when we are in Christ. It is the whole
of creation itself. Of course when creation (particularly the
human creation) turns away from God, it separates itself from
the love of God, and tears itself away from that place where
true life and healing can be found. Yet this idea that creation
came into being in and through the Son means that creation
is also included – it is welcomed into the love of the Father
for the Son. The Spirit's role is therefore not only to draw us
humans into the creative and healing love of God, it is to draw
all of creation into the love of the Father for the Son and the

2. Jn. 7.24; Eph. 1.4

responding love of the Son for the Father. Clark Pinnock writes: 'The Father desires union with the creature as he desires union with the Son. As Christ is a perfect expression of the Father, the creature is called to share in his likeness. In the Son we see what the creature is meant to be.'[3]

The Holy Spirit and a Transformed World

Sometimes a focus on the Holy Spirit can become a dualistic, spiritualising impetus, denying the importance of the ordinary, the physical or the mundane, in favour of the dramatic or ecstatic. This is where a theology that connects the Spirit with creation is important. One of the most distinctive marks of the theology of the Spirit in the Scriptures is the connection made right at the start of the book of Genesis between the Spirit and the created order. The second verse of the whole Bible pictures the Spirit 'brooding' or 'hovering' over the waters at the dawn of creation. Creation in classic Christian theology is *ex nihilo* – in other words, it comes from nothing and without the moment-by-moment sustaining work of the Holy Spirit, would return to nothing. The Holy Spirit is the one who gives and sustains life in all its forms. Nature does not exist on its own, keeping itself going under its own steam, so to speak. It depends on the ongoing work of the Spirit to keep it alive and growing.

There is a key distinction to be made here between two different aspects of the Holy Spirit's work: before and after the fall. In creation, the Spirit works within the world, maintaining and sustaining it by his power, bringing it to its proper fulfilment. After the fall, once the creation has been subjected to frustration, the Spirit has another, additional function, to oppose the spirit of death and destruction, all that seeks to unravel God's good purposes for the world, and instead to renew a decaying world.[4]

---

3. Pinnock, C., *Flame of Love: A Theology of the Holy Spirit* (Downers Grove: Inter-Varsity Press), 58f.
4. For a fuller exploration of this point, see Gunton, C., '"The Spirit Moved over the Face of the Waters": The Holy Spirit and the Created Order', *Spirit of Truth and Power: Studies in Christian Doctrine and Experience*, D. F. Wright (Edinburgh: Rutherford House, 2007), 59–60.

Romans 8, the passage in which Paul writes most fully about the struggles of a broken and damaged creation, also speaks of the Spirit groaning in both that fallen creation and within Christian people as they wait for their 'adoption as sons, the redemption of the body' (Rom. 8.23). This seminal passage for a biblical theology of the Spirit links the Spirit not just to creation, but to the new creation, the resurrection itself. Paul identifies the Spirit as 'the Spirit of him who raised Jesus from the dead' (v. 11). The statement is bursting with theological meaning. It tells us that the resurrection is essentially an event that issues from the heart of God – to use later Trinitarian language, all three persons of the Godhead are involved, and in the light of this insight, God can be identified as the one who raised Jesus in the Spirit.[5] The Spirit does not only sustain the original creation, he brings in the new one.

Both the Holy Spirit (Rom. 8.23) and the resurrection of Jesus (1 Cor. 15.20) are intriguingly described as *aparchē* (απαρχη), 'first fruits' of the age to come. This close connection between the Spirit and the resurrection gives us a vital clue about the role played by the Spirit in the divine economy: that of bringing creation to its fulfilment. God raised Jesus by the Spirit (Rom. 8.1.4; 8.11; 1 Pet. 3.19). Resurrection is what the Spirit does. And resurrection is not just something that happened to the body of Jesus in the first century, it is the destination of all creation. Jesus' resurrection is a foretaste of the full resurrection, not just of all those who are in Christ, but also of the whole created order, which will one day be fully restored and renewed. The Spirit both creates and recreates. He sustains and he renews. One day the creation will be 'liberated from its bondage to decay and brought into the glorious freedom of the children of God' (Rom. 8.21). And just as the Spirit is the one by whom God raised Jesus from death, it is also by the Spirit that God will bring creation to its fulfilment. Not just in the original sense that he gives life that enables created things to grow towards

5. See Fee, G. D., 'Christology and Pneumatology in Romans 8:9–11 – and Elsewhere: Some Reflections on Paul as a Trinitarian' in Green, J. B. and Turner, M., *Jesus of Nazareth: Lord and Christ: Essays on the Historical Jesus and New Testament Christology* (Grand Rapids: Eerdmans, 1994), 312–344.

maturity, but in the additional sense that he heals and restores that which has been damaged and distorted in a broken world. It is because of these themes that the Spirit has often in the history of the church been known as *Creator Spiritus* – Creator Spirit.[6]

In a rich theological exploration of the Holy Spirit, the Roman Catholic theologian Raniero Cantalamessa suggests that the description of the Spirit as Creator affirms the sphere of activity of the Spirit to be the whole of life and creation, not just the life of the believer or the church, and he goes on to highlight the role of the Spirit in bringing creation to its fulfilment or perfection.[7] The Spirit's role in relation to creation is to bring out the fullness or potential latent in the physical creation. This is a classic patristic insight. In the second century, Irenaeus wrote, 'What could the visible fruit of the invisible Spirit be, if not to make flesh mature and receptive of imperishability.'[8] In the fourth century, St Ambrose pointed out that the Spirit transforms creation from something merely utilitarian and functional to something beautiful: 'So when the Spirit was moving upon the water, the creation was without grace; but after this created world underwent the operation of the Spirit, it gained all the beauty of that grace, wherewith the world is illuminated.'[9] Around the same time, Basil the Great wrote of the Spirit's relation to created things: 'He waters them with his life-giving breath and helps them reach their proper fulfilment. He perfects all other things.'[10]

This close relationship between Spirit, creation and new creation/resurrection enables us to see the trajectory of Christian eschatology. The original creation was perfect but not complete: it was just as it should be at the moment it came into being, but like a newborn baby or a bulb planted in the ground, it needed to be brought to full maturity, to fulfilment of all the

6. The Spirit is associated with both creation and new creation in the Old Testament. See e.g. Ps. 104.30; Is. 32.15; Ezk. 37.14.
7. Cantalamessa, R., *Come, Creator Spirit* (Collegeville, Minnesota: Liturgical Press).
8. Irenaeus, *Against Heresies*, 12.3., in Grant, R. M. (ed.) *Irenaeus of Lyons (The Early Church Fathers*, London: Routledge, 1997), 166.
9. Ambrose, *On the Holy Spirit*, II.V.
10. St Basil, *On the Holy Spirit* (Crestwood, New York: St Vladimir's Seminary Press, 1980), 43.

potential that is inherent in it.[11] The animating force, the energy that impels creation to its fulfilment, is the Holy Spirit.

The Spirit enables all that God has created to reach its proper potential, to fulfil all its hopes and possibilities. In the words of Colin Gunton, 'the Spirit is the agent by whom God enables things to become that which they are created to be.'[12] Viewed from the perspective of normal human expectations, the effects of the coming of the Spirit might sometimes look strange, unworldly and disturbing – flames of fire alighting on heads, ecstatic languages spoken, and prophetic words uttered do not seem very 'normal'. However, viewed from the wider perspective of God's purpose for creation, when the Spirit is truly at work, created things do not go off on a tangent, becoming odd or eccentric. Rather they become more fully themselves as they were originally created with the potential to be. Of course there are many things in the church and the world that claim to be the work of the Spirit that are indeed very odd and eccentric, but biblically speaking a true sign of the work of the Spirit is when the hidden latent quality in any person, or indeed any created thing, emerges and is drawn out. In fact no one and nothing in creation can reach that potential without the work of the Spirit. The spiritualising tendency that implies that reality is only found in moments of ecstasy when the visible and tangible world is left behind is a long way from a biblical, Christian understanding of the Spirit. The Spirit comes to transform, to mature life in all its dimensions – the body, the workplace, the environment, the economy – everything. Michael Welker's major work on the theology of the Spirit, one of the most important contributions to pneumatology in the last twenty years, stresses exactly this point. The Spirit cannot be confined to numinous experiences and extraordinary gifts, however important they might be. Instead, the Spirit is given to transform real human life in all its dimensions: 'Exaltation and illumination of the Spirit means nothing less than that real

11. For exploration of this point see Gunton, C., *The Christian Faith: An Introduction to Christian Doctrine* (Oxford: Blackwell, 2002), 19; and Wright, N. T., *Surprised by Hope* (London: SPCK, 2007), 114.
12. Gunton, C., 'The Spirit Moved over the Face of the Waters', 70.

fleshly life is enabled by the Spirit and in the Spirit to be the place where God's glory is made present.'[13]

In the light of the last chapter, it is clear precisely how this task is fulfilled: the generous, prodigal Spirit draws creation back into the sphere of the love of the Father for the Son, into the realm of the kingdom of God, which is the kingdom of love. We know from studies of childhood and parenthood how significant an atmosphere of love is for healthy growth and development. A child who grows up knowing she is loved is more likely to be a balanced, stable and productive person than someone whose childhood lacks love or affirmation. We saw in the last chapter how Jesus' deep sense of security derives theologically from the love of the Father for the Son, issuing in the deep trust the Father has for him. Love is creative. It liberates, reassures and trusts. It also enables people to reach their full potential. An unloved child often turns out to be an emotionally, spiritually and perhaps even physically diminished adult. Just as a child can only grow into its full potential in an atmosphere of love, so the creation itself only reaches fulfillment when it is drawn into the love at the heart of God: the love of the Father for the Son. It is as God turns his face towards creation in love that the Spirit renews the face of the earth (Ps. 104.29–30).[14]

The Spirit and the Future

The Spirit will bring about a new creation. However, this is not just a promise or a pledge, it is a reality that has begun in the world here and now. We have already noticed how Romans 8.23 speaks of the 'firstfruits of the Spirit', experienced by Christian believers as they wait for their adoption as God's children. This is the Greek word *aparchē* (απαρχη), the first bluebell of spring, the first apple on the tree, the first shoots of a crop soon

13. Welker, M., *God the Spirit* (Minneapolis: Fortress, 1994), 330.
14. Ellington, S. A., 'The Face of God as His Creating Spirit' in Yong, A. (ed.), *The Spirit Renews the Face of the Earth* (Eugene, Oregon: Pickwick, 2009) explores a fascinating link between the face of God and the Spirit of God turned towards creation: 'Life is only sustainable in the continued presence of and with the enduring spirit of God.' (16)

to be harvested. Ephesians 1.13–14 suggests another image for the Spirit – the 'deposit [*arrabōn* (αρραβων)] guaranteeing our inheritance.' 2 Corinthians 1.22 has the same idea, as does 2 Corinthians 5.5: 'he has … put his Spirit in our hearts as a first instalment, guaranteeing what is to come.'

The point of these two images is striking. In the present, we are not just given a pledge or a promise that the creation will one day be renewed, and that all things will one day be made new (Rev. 21.5), we are offered more. We are given an actual foretaste of that day, the experience of it here and now in the present. The significance of the first bluebell of spring or the first apple on the tree lies not just in itself but in what it signifies – the change of season that is coming. Yet at the same time the bluebell and the apple are not just empty signs, they are actually part of the harvest or springtime that is to come. They are the real thing, not just a pointer to the real thing.

If I owe someone a hundred pounds, and I am determined to pay them back, there are two ways I can signify my intentions. One is to issue an IOU – a piece of paper that says that I will pay it back one day. This is a start, but in itself, the piece of paper is worth nothing. It is just a sign. It is a useful sign, as it promises repayment, but at the end of the day it cannot be taken into a shop and spent. Another way is to give a downpayment of ten pounds as a pledge that I will one day deliver the rest. This is different. It is a sign, but it is much more. It is part of the fullness of what is to come. It can actually be taken to a shop and spent – it is the real thing. Not the whole of it, but real nonetheless.

This is the point being made in these texts and in the use of these words. The Holy Spirit is more than a pledge or a promise. In the gift of the Spirit we are given an actual experience of the age to come, a taste of the new creation. It is not just an empty sign, it is a taste of the future resurrection life brought into the present.

There is a basic dualism found in many New Testament writings. It is found in passages such as 1 Corinthians 2.14f;

3.1; 15.44–46. It is essentially the distinction between the
'spiritual', *pneuma* (πνευμα), and the 'natural', *psuchē* (ψυχη),
or sometimes 'fleshly', *sarx* (σαρζ). These words are translated
in different ways in different versions of the Bible, but it is
tempting, especially using the English words 'spiritual' and
'physical'[15] to think of this as a spirit–body dualism, one that
draws a sharp distinction between the immaterial world of
spirit and the physical world of flesh and matter, or even the
(good) supernatural realm and the (less good) natural realm.
Such a view is common, yet in the light of this future-oriented
theology of the Spirit, the distinction is clearly intended as an
eschatological rather than a material or ontological dualism.
The vital distinction being drawn is not between the spirit and
the body, but between the present and the future. The presence
of the Spirit is not an escape from the world, but the presence of
the world's future in anticipation.

In 1 Corinthians 2–3, Paul is not depicting one person living
with a mind to immaterial spiritual realities while another is
preoccupied with mundane material objects. That would be
Platonism, not Christianity. Paul's contrast is instead between
the person who is animated purely by the normal human
life force, biological life or *psuchē*, and another person who is
animated by something further – the life of the Holy Spirit,
pneuma – which is a wholly additional dimension of reality,
hidden from the life of *psuchē*, but every bit as real.[16] The same
is true of the distinction between the 'natural' body and the
'resurrection body' described in 1 Corinthians 15. It is not that
resurrection bodies are immaterial or ghostly spectres. They
are real bodies, not half-real shadows. They are bodies fully
suffused by the Spirit, not just by biological life. If anything,
they are more real not less, a point that C.S. Lewis memorably
tried to convey in *The Great Divorce* with his image of grass and
trees in the new creation that were 'so much solider than things
in our country, that men were ghosts by comparison.'[17]

This seems to have been taken for granted in early

---

15. 1 Cor. 15.44 (NRSV).
16. Wright, *Surprised by Hope*.
17. Lewis, C. S., *The Great Divorce* (London: Geoffrey Bles., 1946).

Christianity. Irenaeus makes the distinction between the temporary fleeting nature of *psuchē*, and the eternal nature of *pneuma*: 'The breath of life that makes the man psychic, is one thing, and the life giving Spirit is another ... breath is something temporary, while Spirit is eternal. And breath grows for a moment and stays for a time and then goes away, leaving breathless what was in it before; but Spirit, possessing a man inside and outside, always remains and will never leave him.'[18] The Holy Spirit creates in us something new and different from what is natural – it brings us into the realm of the supernatural, although it is vital not to push this distinction too far. The 'supernatural' is not in opposition to the natural, but builds on it and completes it.

Karl Barth was right in his insistence that 'the Holy Spirit is not a form of the human Spirit ... the Holy Spirit is not identical with the human spirit, but he meets it.'[19] The Holy Spirit cannot be collapsed into human psychology as a dimension of human 'spirituality' as Schleiermacher and all who have followed him have tended to do. The Holy Spirit does not simply denote the 'spiritual' side of general human nature as opposed to the physical or mental. It is a different dimension of being altogether, as this eschatological dualism present in the New Testament makes clear.

The Spirit brings the future into the present. The presence of the Spirit is a foretaste of what will come in the new age, the day when God's love will reign, when he will make all things new, when he will bring the project of creation to its wonderful fulfilment. The Spirit therefore brings within human reach a new dimension, which from one angle is called resurrection and from another, the kingdom of God. This new dimension of reality has within it a new way of being, a new rationality and a new order. This is what Paul is driving at in 1 Corinthians 2, when he contrasts the 'wisdom of this age' with 'God's secret wisdom ... not in words taught us by human wisdom, but in

18. Grant, *Irenaeus of Lyons*, 165.
19. Barth, K., *Dogmatics in Outline* (London: SCM, 1985).

words taught by the Spirit.'[20] The Spirit as both a guarantee and a foretaste of the new creation brings into the range of human possibilities a new rationality, a new way of thinking, a new order that is both continuous with, yet goes beyond our normal human rationality. This new way of thinking and processing knowledge is accessed by faith rather than unaided reason, yet this is not to say it is irrational – it simply follows a different and transfigured rationality.

This new world of thought, action and behaviour has perhaps best been described by the poets and storytellers rather than a more prosaic type of scientist and theologian. It is a world best accessed by faith and imagination, which can in turn renew and heal our 'normal' rationality. It is a wisdom that Dante tried to describe in the *Divine Comedy*, Bunyan in his *Pilgrim's Progress* and C.S. Lewis in the Narnia stories. This new rationality comes into play when the future arrives in the present, when that which God has prepared for those who love him, that which 'no eye has seen, no ear has heard, no mind has conceived' comes within reach of us through the Holy Spirit (1 Cor. 2.9).

The Kingdom of God

In the teaching of Jesus, this new dimension of reality is described as the kingdom of God. For Jesus, this term takes its content from Old Testament theology and its expectation of a final end to Israel's exile and the coming of God's kingdom. If one thing has become clear in recent scholarship on the kingdom of God, it is that the kingdom Jesus expected was not life after death, or some otherworldly reality, but a transfiguration of this life and this world. He and all first-century Jews looked forward not to the destruction of the

---

20. 1 Cor. 2.6–16. It is clear that Paul is not talking here of a kind of 'gnostic' body of knowledge kept secret, only for the initiated. This is not a normal human knowledge whose only distinction is that it is kept secret from ordinary people – it is a new dimension of knowledge taught only by the Spirit. See Witherington III, B., *Jesus the Sage: The Pilgrimage of Wisdom* (Edinburgh: T. & T. Clark, 1985), 299. See also Horsley, R. A., 'Gnosis in Corinth: 1 Corinthians 8.1–6' *NTS* 27 (1980): 32–51, esp. 32.

creation and the end of the space–time universe, but its renewal; not to escaping the body and the physical creation, but to its re-creation under the visible rule of God. The message of the kingdom was not primarily an invitation to life after death, but the announcement of a new reality that had come about in the life and work of Jesus. As N.T. Wright puts it: 'the announcement of the kingdom of God could never ... be heard as a "timeless" message, an incidental example or occurrence of some general truth. The whole point was that Israel's dream was coming true *right now*.'[21]

The kingdom is the subject of potentially endless definition, but perhaps the simplest description is 'the realm where God has his way'. In the kingdom of God, everything happens according to God's desire and will. It is where God's rule and reign are visible for all to see. In the kingdom of God, the enemies of God's creative work are overcome, and the powers that would seek to destroy life and creation are defeated. When the kingdom comes, the sick are healed, the addicts are freed, the hungry are fed, the aimless find purpose, the guilty find forgiveness, the dead are raised, and the creation is healed. When related to his teaching on the kingdom of God, Jesus' miracles become much more significant than we might have thought. They are not tricks to impress people or to compel belief, but rather have a striking theological meaning given by Jesus' announcement of the main purpose of his ministry: to bring in the kingdom of God (Mk. 1.15). This announcement of the kingdom in the teaching of Jesus reflected his belief that God was making a radical new move in salvation history – that in some sense, Israel's exile was coming to an end, God was setting up his kingdom in the world and a new phase in God's relation to the world had begun.

When Jesus announces that in him the kingdom of God has come near, the natural thing to do is to look for the signs that he is telling the truth: where is the evidence that God's will is finally being done 'on earth as it is in heaven'? The evidence lies precisely in the actions of Jesus. When Jesus heals the sick,

21. Wright, N. T., *Jesus and the Victory of God* (London: SPCK, 1996).

raises the dead, multiplies bread to feed the hungry and invites despised tax collectors to join him, these are the signs of the kingdom. In Luke 7, the disciples of John the Baptist approach Jesus with the question of whether he is the Messiah, the one who was to come to bring in the kingdom, or whether they should be waiting for someone else. The answer is not a bold claim to be the Christ, nor a hesitant quizzical answer. It is effectively, 'see for yourself':

> At that very time Jesus cured many who had diseases, sicknesses and evil spirits, and gave sight to many who were blind. So he replied to the messengers, 'Go back and report to John what you have seen and heard: The blind receive sight, the lame walk, those who have leprosy are cured, the deaf hear, the dead are raised, and the good news is preached to the poor. Blessed is the man who does not fall away on account of me.'

Luke 7.21–23

The miracles of Jesus are the emphatic signs that in him the kingdom of God has come, at least in part. It is as if, in the space around the person of Jesus of Nazareth for those brief years of his public ministry, you could see the kingdom of God coming before your very eyes.

Sometimes the impression is given that the main thing in the ministry of Jesus was his teaching. The miracles of Jesus were at best illustrations of his teaching and at worst, distractions from it. The understanding of the ministry of Jesus and its context in the kingdom of God we have been exploring suggests that the relationship between Jesus' actions and words is quite different. Jesus was not primarily a teacher of religious truth. Although Jesus gave a revolutionary interpretation of the law, the most significant thing in his ministry was not a new teaching he brought to the world, but a new reality – the kingdom of God, or a new creation. In fact, the miracles of Jesus are seen as a kind of new creation – the restoration of creation to its original wholeness and friendliness, as God becomes king again over his creation, even in this limited yet startling way in the time and space around Jesus of Nazareth. This kingdom was seen in his actions, particularly his miracles, where God had his way in bringing justice, healing, life and beauty, at the same time as overcoming death, disease, injustice and cynicism. His words can bring life and healing. Yet his more discursive teaching by and large is a commentary on his actions: his words explain the significance of what is happening in his ministry.[22] This is seen in an exchange recorded in all three synoptic gospels, but which stands out most clearly in Matthew's version. After Jesus restores sight and speech to a 'blind and dumb' man, the Pharisees accuse him of performing this miracle by the power of Beelzebub, a popular Jewish term for a senior demon deriving from the old Canaanite god Ba-al. Jesus replies:

> Every kingdom divided against itself will be ruined, and every city or household divided against itself will not stand. If Satan drives out Satan, he is divided against himself. How then can his kingdom stand? And if I drive out demons by Beelzebub, by whom do your people drive them out? So then, they will be your judges. But if I drive out demons by the Spirit of God, then the kingdom of God has come upon you.

Matthew 12.25–28

There are two key points to be made here. The first is that Jesus' words explain directly the significance of his actions – they mean that the kingdom of God has come, and the scribes and the Pharisees need to read the signs of the times. This indicates the theological relationship between the words and actions of Jesus and therefore, the words and actions of his followers. Jesus is not just a preacher. He is a worker of miracles. The world is not saved through his words but through his actions – in particular his death and resurrection. The words however

---

22. C. H. Dodd's well-known distinction may be helpful here, between Jesus' *kerygma* – the announcement of the kingdom that has power to heal and bring life – and his *didache*, the explanation of the significance of the miracles, whether brought about by speech or gesture.

remain vital. Jesus' teaching explains the meaning of the things
that Jesus does. How would we know the significance of the
healings of the sick, the feeding of hungry crowds, the raising of
Lazarus and the son of the widow of Nain, if we were not told it
by Jesus?

The second point however is the explicit link made in the
teaching of Jesus between the signs of the kingdom (in this
case the driving out of demonic powers, and the restoration
of life-giving sight and speech) and the Holy Spirit. It is by
the Holy Spirit that Jesus performs the signs of the kingdom.
Entry into the kingdom is by the Holy Spirit (Jn. 3.5). In a
sense the kingdom can even be described as life in the Spirit. St
Paul makes the link: 'For the kingdom of God is not a matter
of eating and drinking, but of righteousness, peace and joy in
the Holy Spirit' (Rom. 14.17). The Spirit's life is central to the
kingdom of God. The Spirit brings about the anticipation of
resurrection life here and now, which is nothing less than a
preview or foretaste of life in the kingdom of God.

The link between Jesus, the kingdom and the Spirit is at
its clearest in the baptism stories, which we have already
examined. Jesus receives the baptism of John, but unlike most
recipients of this rite, as it takes place he also receives the
Spirit in a very obvious and manifest way, an event whose
significance is indicated in that unusually it is attested in all
four gospels (Mt. 3.16; Mk. 1.10; Lk. 3.22; Jn. 1.32f). The Spirit
comes on Jesus as a testimony to his sonship of the Father –
'You are my son, whom I love; with you I am well pleased.'
(Mk. 1.10) – but also to indicate the beginning of his public
ministry, his inauguration of the kingdom of God.

The Kingdom and the Spirit

Jesus' primary calling was to bring in the kingdom of God,
through his life, death and resurrection. Naturally speaking,

this is only a partial coming. Although the signs of the kingdom are present, Herod, Pontius Pilate and Caesar are still enthroned in the seats of power. Sickness, sin and death still stalk the land. This is the presence of a kingdom 'present yet future, already established yet needing still to win its decisive victory.'[23] The kingdom in the ministry of Jesus is a reality, yet it is also an anticipation. It is the same as we saw in the relationship between the Spirit and the resurrection: the activity of Jesus is a foretaste of the kingdom that is coming, just as the experience of the earliest churches of the Spirit of God in their life together is a foretaste of the eschatological future: these are both ways of essentially saying the same thing. The common denominator is life in the Spirit, the Spirit who came upon Jesus at his baptism, not to make him the Son of God in any adoptionist sense, as if he was not God's Son until then, but to empower him for the ministry of the kingdom.[24]

When Jesus is present, and therefore by definition when the kingdom is 'at hand' (Mk. 1.14f; Mt. 4.17), a number of things happen. There is the possibility of experience of the immanent presence of God in the person of Jesus, an experience that can bring both joy and holy fear. There is the reality of transformation of the created order: bodies are healed as Jesus cures the lame, the deaf and the blind. Scarcity of food turns into enough for everyone as five thousand are fed from one packed lunch. Outsiders are brought in as lepers are healed. Water that threatens to drown and destroy becomes supportive and co-operative as Jesus treads on it. The kingdom always has this sense of the presence of God in power, and the resulting transformation of the world. The two are vitally linked. The kingdom is the presence of God that in itself brings about change in the world. The kingdom brings into human experience 'God's empowering presence', as Gordon Fee describes Paul's pneumatology.[25]

The kingdom of God is what happens when the Spirit

23. Wright, *Jesus and the Victory of God*, 468.
24. Luke's version of the baptism of Jesus makes this clear by establishing the link between the baptism and the beginning of the public ministry of Jesus (see Lk. 3.22–23).
25. Fee, G. D., *God's Empowering Presence: the Holy Spirit in the Letters of Paul* (Peabody, MA: Hendrickson Publishers, 1994).

comes. And to put it conversely, the kingdom cannot come unless the Spirit comes, any more than Jesus could do what he did without the Spirit coming upon him and working through him. As Paul is at pains to point out, 'the kingdom of God is not a matter of talk but of power' (1 Cor. 4.20). The kingdom has practical, actual demonstration. It is no ethereal concept, but can be seen and experienced – and the same is true of the Spirit. When the Spirit brings the creation into the fulfilment of its potential, we see God's will being done within the world. The true sign of the Spirit will therefore be a renewed experience of the presence and love of God *and* the beginnings of real transformation in both personal lives and the whole created order. Both are vital. A fresh experience of God's love without a corresponding impulse to heal a broken world could be purely spiritual narcissism, an inner feeling that might just be wishful thinking or self-indulgent emotionalism. Social activism without a fresh experience of being brought into the love of God is valuable, but lacks the sense of freedom, persistence and playfulness that comes from being rooted in the love of God rather than fitful and erratic human determination. As St Symeon the New Theologian puts it, echoing the great spiritual and theological tradition on this point: 'the grace of the Spirit will not remain with us without the practice of the commandments, nor will the practice of the commandments serve any useful purpose without the grace of God.'[26] The acts of the kingdom come from the presence of the Spirit.

If the Spirit heals creation by drawing it back into the love that pulses at the heart of God, the love between the Father and the Son, and if the life of the Spirit is at the very centre of this kingdom, then the nature of this kingdom becomes clearer: it is the kingdom of the love of God. It is the place where God's love has free reign to be known, experienced and to work its healing and restoring power. The Spirit works to bring us and all creation back into the love of God, and the result is both an

---

26. Palmer, G. E. H.; Sherrard, P.; et al. (eds.), *The Philokalia: The Complete Text, compiled by St Nikodemos of the Holy Mountain and St Makarios of Corinth* (London: Faber & Faber, 1995).

experience of the love of God in Christ, and also transformation in the communities and environment around us. Both are the work of the Spirit

The Spirit and Human Vocation

This suggests another dimension to the significance of the Spirit's uniting us with Christ. Not only does it mean that we know the love of the Father for the Son, it also means that we find ourselves called into the mission of the Son towards the world. Being 'in Christ' by the Spirit[27] means becoming caught up in his work to prepare for the new creation. Our new *identity* leads to a new *vocation*, to join with God in his work of 'bringing all things together under Christ',[28] 'looking forward to a new heaven and a new earth'.[29]

The Spirit does not do his work in creation directly. Alongside the Spirit, humanity plays a distinct role in the creation stories in the development and maturing of creation. As human beings are created at the climax of creation, they are called to 'work it, and take care of it' (Gn. 2.15). Humanity is deeply involved in God's work to bring creation to its fulfillment, through activities such as work, art, technology and the scientific enterprise of understanding, naming and harnessing the powers of the world.[30] The Spirit of God is free to work without human agency (after all, flowers grow, birds sing and forests breathe without the help of people), yet to bring creation to its true fulfillment, the Spirit works through human agency. Humanity always had a purpose. It was to work with the Holy Spirit in caring for the created order, and enabling it to fulfill the latent potential in it. Parents cannot make a child mature. They can however help to shape the child as he grows, forming his mind, interests, values and future career. Gardeners cannot make plants grow. They can however

---

27. Eph. 1.13.
28. Eph. 1.10.
29. 2 Pet. 3.13.
30. This dimension will be explored further in Chapter 6.

tend the plant, pruning it and fertilising the soil to make sure it grows straight and free from parasites. In the same way, humanity cannot bring or give life to the creation – only God the Holy Spirit does that. Yet we can, and are called to, shape that creation as it develops, giving it form, order and structure.

When we remember the second function of the Spirit within a damaged, broken world, we see a further role for humanity. Our calling is not only to help creation grow to maturity, but also to be involved in its healing. Of course, humanity itself is affected by that brokenness. We were intended to be involved in the evolving growth of creation into maturity, yet we have become part of the problem, damaging and destroying the very creation we were meant to tend and care for. Every harsh word, broken relationship or polluted river is evidence that we are complicit in the destruction of creation, joining in the impulse to return creation to the chaos from which it came, co-operating with forces of death, not the Spirit who brings Life.

The work of redemption requires forgiveness, cleansing, and a new creation, so that we can again take our place, working with, rather than against the Spirit in his mission to bring life and vitality to the world. The sending of the incarnate Son restores the image of God in humanity, and atones for the sins of the world. Paul puts it like this: 'In Christ, God was reconciling the world to himself' (2 Cor. 5.19). God's work of restoring the broken creation is focused in the coming of the divine Son into the world in the person of Jesus the Christ. If the Spirit is to work with us and through us to enable creation to reach its full potential, that means that humans will not only need to be ransomed and forgiven, they will also need to be filled with that same Spirit, so they can be agents of God's work in the world. The Incarnation suggests that God's normal way of working is not to use people like instruments, like a workman using a screwdriver or a gardener a spade. Jesus has his own will, which he chooses to bend to the Father's will, as happens most tellingly in Gethsemane. God transforms from within, gradually changing desire and will, so that people choose to do his will, rather than being forced to. So, for us to be agents of the Spirit's work of completing creation, we need to be filled with that same Spirit, not just mechanically used by him. We are filled with the Spirit so that he can work through us to complete his work in the world.

There is a sobering side to this too. A sense of the power of the Spirit and the overpowering sense of the love of God can sometimes create a one-sided triumphalism. However, being united with Christ does not just mean knowing the love of the Father, it also means being united with him 'in his death' (Rom. 6.5). We recall that Romans 8, examined in the last chapter, contained that solemn note of suffering hidden within its theology of the Spirit:

> The Spirit himself testifies with our spirit that we are God's children. Now if we are children, then we are heirs –heirs of God and co-heirs with Christ, *if indeed we share in his sufferings* in order that we may also share in his glory.

Romans 8.15–17

If we are united with Christ through the Spirit, so that we experience for ourselves the intimate love of the Father for his Son, enabling us to call him 'Abba' as Jesus did, then this text reminds us that we are united with the crucified Son. Our fellowship with Christ is a fellowship of his sufferings (Phil. 3.10).

Recalling Charlie Mackesy's sculpture of the Prodigal Son that served as the starting point for our explorations, the Son held tight by the Father is the suffering Son, helpless, at the end of his resources, yet embraced and raised to life by the loving embrace of the Father. It is that very Son with whom we are united by the prodigal Spirit. That means that Christian experience will involve *both* a deep and intimate knowledge of the love of the Father, an overpowering, healing and affirming sense of being loved and trusted, *and* also involve sharing in the suffering of the Son Jesus for the sake of his world.

The cross is the shape that the love of God takes in a fallen world. When the world turns away from the God whose Spirit gives life, it chooses the opposite: death. Because God loves the world so much that he is determined not to abandon it to its fate, he chooses to enter that world in human form to take upon himself the consequences of that fateful human choice, to triumph over it once and for all, to open the way back to life. That is what God's love does. Without the fall, the incarnation would surely still have happened, as creation was always intended as the arena for the coming of God, yet it would not have resulted in a cross. The cross only becomes necessary as the inevitable outcome of God entering a broken world not just to complete and crown it but to heal it of its wounds, to overcome the consequences of its rebellion. Naturally we are not called to die for the sins of the world. We do not overcome death by our death. However, if we are truly to become one with Christ, that will not only mean knowing of the love of the Father, it will also involve a vocation to join in some way in his sufferings for the healing of the world (Rom. 8.17; Col. 1.24). Our attempts to be the channels of God's salvation to the world through acts of kindness, mercy, forgiveness, alleviating poverty, washing ugly wounds, cleaning smelly drains, visiting awkward neighbours and so on will at times be hard, tiresome, even painful. And yet that is the shape that love takes in a fallen world. It is as we enter into the suffering of a broken world, as we become one with the crucified Christ in the Spirit, 'sharing in his sufferings' that we know the fullness of the Father's love, so that we can also know his resurrection life. This is the paradox of divine love: a true *pneumatologia crucis*.[31] To pray the prayer 'Come Holy Spirit' is a wonderful, but perhaps also a sombre thing to do. It is wonderful because it asks God to draw

---

31. See Moltmann, J., *The Spirit of Life: A Universal Affirmation* (London: SCM, 1992); Dabney, D. L., 'Naming the Spirit: Towards a Pneumatology of the Cross', in Preece, G. and Pickard, S., *Starting with the Spirit* (Hindmarsh: Australian Theological Forum), 28–59. See 69–71 for further discussion of this point.

us into the same relationship of love that Jesus had with the
Father. It is sombre because it is asking God to draw us into the
same relationship Jesus had with the world, which led him to
a cross. When the Spirit unites us with Christ, he beckons us to
walk on the path blazed by the divine Son of God, through the
cross to resurrection, a path that ends at the right hand of God,
with Christ 'in his glory' (Rom. 8.17).

The human vocation after the fall is not just to develop and
harness the powers of creation, being filled with the Spirit to
bring beauty and order out of disorder and unruly growth.
It is also to be involved in the healing of creation. And that
involvement will bring suffering as well as glory. We reach our
potential and creation reaches its potential only through the
love that chooses to suffer for the beloved's sake. The filling of
the Spirit in us will bring a deep knowledge of both the love of
the Father and the suffering of the Son.

The Spirit unites us with Christ so that we have the same
relationship as he has with the Father, but also the same
relationship as he has with the world. Being 'in Christ' entails
drawing us into the ecstasy of the divine love, and the agony of
engagement with a suffering and hurting creation.

The Church and the Kingdom of God

The Holy Spirit brings the creation to its fulfilment. The Spirit
therefore brings about an anticipation of the end, a foretaste
of the future. The church can thus be understood as the
community of people filled with the Holy Spirit, and dedicated
to the agenda of the kingdom of God as manifest in the ministry
of Jesus. It is, as more catholic Christians often like to say, an
extension of the incarnation, not primarily in the institutional
sense, but in the sense that it is defined by its calling to do
what Jesus did: to anticipate, to point forward to, and to
provide glimpses and signs of the kingdom, the new creation

that one day will come.[32] The church is not the kingdom – any
experience of the frailty and imperfection of the average church
acts as an all too vivid reminder of that – but it always has
the kingdom as its goal and purpose. An individual church is
a local expression of this new reality brought into the world
on the day when the Spirit came, the day of Pentecost. And
because of the close relationship we have been exploring here
between the Spirit, the kingdom and the new creation, church
is the place where this new reality can be both experienced and
identified.

The sure sign of the work of the Spirit in the church as the
community of the kingdom is its outworking in these two
ways – the manifest presence of God and the transformation of
his world. In Romans 8, the Spirit groans inwardly in us as we
wait for 'our adoption as sons, the redemption of our bodies'
(v. 23). Yet in the midst of this frustration, we are promised the
actual presence and reality of the Spirit, which is a real taste of
the future in the present. A church that wants to take part in
God's work in the world will have both a conscious longing for
the presence and power of God and a determination to see the
renewal of the created order. Evangelism, as we shall explore
further in chapter four, therefore needs to be understood as part
of a wider agenda of renovation, or the coming of the kingdom.
The goal is not just to see individuals converted, so that they
are happier and more fulfilled, but to see the recalibration of
individual hearts and lives that they become agents of change
and compassion – enlisted in the agenda of the kingdom, the
renewal of creation, drawn back into the loving heart of God. It
is in this sense a movement of repentance in the New Testament
sense of *metanoia* – the turning around of lives towards
involvement in the mission of God to heal, restore and renew
the world.

These two themes – the empowering experience of the love
of God through the Spirit, the future in the present, and the

---

32. Moltmann writes: 'An anticipation is not yet a fulfilment. But it is already the presence of the
future in the conditions of history.' Moltmann, J., *The Church in the Power of the Spirit: a Contribution
of Messianic Ecclesiology* (London: SCM Press, 1977), 193.

often painful involvement in the process of transformation in a broken world – will run through the rest of this book. But is experience of God possible? Is it really part of classical Christian faith? The next chapter begins to explore that very question.

CHAPTER 3

THE HOLY SPIRIT AND EXPERIENCE

So far we have been exploring human identity and human vocation. We have developed Christian answers to the questions of who we are, and what we are here for. The prodigal Spirit, the one who reaches out from the heart of God to draw all creation back into his healing and life-giving presence, gives us a new sense of self and a new purpose for living. However, it is one thing to lay out these answers as theories in a book, and quite another to know them intimately and existentially, in actual experience. How do we come to know who we are? How do we begin to act out our vocation in the world? In more sophisticated language, these are the questions of epistemology.

There is a basic epistemology within Christian theology that says we know by faith and not by sight (2 Cor. 5.7; Heb. 11.1) and that faith is a gift of God through the Holy Spirit (Ephesians 2.8). Faith comes about through a variety of means, including the testimony of Scripture, intellectual enquiry and personal experience. This chapter explores the particular role of the last of these – the idea that faith involves a tangible experience of the reality of God, and specifically an experience of the love of God as we have been exploring in the past few chapters, an experience that can take a wide variety of forms, but which nonetheless is real and effective. It goes on to examine the relationship of experience to the theological themes of the Spirit, the Trinity and the kingdom, which have occupied us so far. It suggests that we find our identity and our vocation through an encounter with God through the Holy Spirit.

Ever since the eighteenth century, theology has been living in the shadow of the problems raised by Immanuel Kant over our knowledge of God. Kant's famous distinction between the *Ding-an-Sich* – the 'thing in itself' – and the *Bild* – the subjective image we have of that thing in our minds – brought a new level of self-consciousness to our perception of the world. All we can be sure of is that we have a perception in our minds of the world outside. We cannot ultimately be sure that that image is the same as the real world. We do not ultimately have access to the 'noumenal' world out there, only the 'phenomenal' world as we experience it. We are, according to Kant, trapped in subjectivity.

This critique also of course extends to our knowledge of God. Can we be sure that we know God himself? Or do we just have our subjective experience of him? It was this distinction that led Schleiermacher to re-cast theology in the language of human experience, giving up on the possibility or relevance of direct and objective knowledge of God, and restarting the theological project with human experience rather than divine revelation to us. The problem is not so much whether God reveals himself, as whether we have the apparatus to receive that revelation. God might well have revealed himself in Christ and in the Scriptures, but if we can only access a subjective appreciation of that revelation, it still leaves us falling short of sure, true, objective knowledge of God. It is like TV reception – there might be a TV signal out there, broadcasting programmes into the ether, but if I do not have a TV set with a properly configured aerial to receive it, the existence of the signal is irrelevant and useless to me.

The question then becomes a matter of the status of our

experience of God. Is it 'merely' human experience, locked into subjectivity? Or can it claim something more? This is where a doctrine of the Holy Spirit is so important. St Paul writes of how the Spirit of God bears witness with our human spirit that we are children of God (Rom. 8.16). The Holy Spirit intercedes for us and within us (8.26). In other words, here is a claim that the gift of the Spirit is the gift of the ability to encounter God himself. The Holy Spirit gives us the ability, the apparatus if you like, to receive the revelation of God and to have direct, personal knowledge of God. In the Spirit, we are given what we need for direct access to God's revelation in Christ and the Scriptures. Without the Spirit, in a sense, all we have is information. As Calvin puts it: 'until our minds become intent upon the Spirit, Christ, so to speak, lies idle because we coldly contemplate him as outside ourselves'[1], and 'Paul shows the Spirit to be the inner teacher by whose effort the promise of salvation penetrates into our minds, a promise that would otherwise only strike the air or beat upon our ears.'[2] In other words the Spirit enables encounter, making possible a personal, direct knowledge of God that goes beyond the merely subjective and uncertain. The Spirit, contrary to what is sometimes thought, is not merely about subjective experience, but when combined with the revelation of God in Christ and through the Scriptures, makes possible objective, true knowledge of God.

Furthermore, the patristic insistence that the Spirit is not a created spirit, but every bit as divine as the Father and the Son, is in fact a claim that in experience of the Spirit, it is truly *God* that we experience. It is not merely subjective, locked into the uncertain realm of the human spirit where we cannot be sure of exactly what we are experiencing, but it is an actual engagement with God himself.

In the last chapter, we considered the eschatological dualism that is found in the New Testament between the life of *psuchē* (ψυχη) and of *pneuma* (πνευμα). The New Testament writers see

1. *Institutes*, III.3.
2. *Institutes*, III.4.

the Spirit as more than a notional idea or a theological principle. The Spirit is a real foretaste of the age to come, God in dynamic action, 'God's empowering presence' as Gordon Fee called it.[3] This is the power of resurrection, a new creation. When we see the significance of the Spirit in overcoming the prison of subjectivity, and grasp the force of this eschatological dualism, it is hard to avoid the conclusion that the life into which the Spirit brings us is intended to be *experienced*. The first chapter examined Trinitarian theology, suggesting that the Spirit brings us into the love between the Father and the Son. The notion that the heart of reality, the heart of God can be described as the love between a parent and a child, surely indicates that this is intended to be felt and experienced, no less than, and perhaps even more than, human love is felt and experienced. When the Spirit initiates us into the love between the Father and the Son, which is the destiny of all of creation that chooses to be included in it, it is to be expected that something is actually *felt* – it will not pass unnoticed.

In fact, this is one of the defining aspects of the work of the Spirit. In the context of Israel's exile, Ezekiel, the Old Testament prophet who speaks most of the Spirit, uses a striking and memorable image: 'I will … put a new spirit in them; I will remove from them their heart of stone and give them a heart of flesh' (Ezk. 11.19). It is an image of the return of feeling to a spiritually numb soul. A heart that could not feel anything for God, for people, for the suffering of the world, begins to feel the painful tingling of renewed sensation, a new set of experiences that reconnect it to God and to the world.

Jürgen Moltmann's *The Spirit of Life* was a bold reaffirmation of the importance of experience of the Spirit in Christian life and action. Reacting to Barthian dialectical theology's wariness of experience, a fear that led to oxymoronic 'revelations that cannot be experienced',[4] Moltmann insisted that a proper eschatological dualism, rather than the more Platonic dualism

3. Fee, G. D., *God's Empowering Presence: the Holy Spirit in the Letters of Paul* (Peabody, MA: Hendrickson, 1994).
4. Moltmann, J., *The Spirit of Life: A Universal Affirmation* (London: SCM, 1992), 7.

of time and eternity that Barth espoused, would lead to the rehabilitation of the possibility of true experience of the Spirit. If the Spirit is located in a world outside time (as Barth implied) it is hard to see how we can access that world directly – we can only point to it through the proclamation of the church. However, if the Spirit is a downpayment of the coming kingdom, to come on earth as it is in heaven, giving us a foretaste of the future kingdom now, it is easier to see how the Spirit can be experienced under the conditions of the present.

It is hard to read the *Confessions* of St Augustine, the mystical writings of Gregory of Nyssa, the visions of St Teresa or the letters of Samuel Rutherford without a sense that experience and emotion are an integral part of true Christian faith. However, there have been times when such emotion and experience have been profoundly distrusted. The eighteenth-century Enlightenment was such a time. It had some cause for doing so, emerging out of the experience of the various European wars of the seventeenth century in which faith played at least some role. The early modern period had bequeathed a divided Europe, with the emerging nation states jostling for power, and often using religious and theological markers to define and defend themselves in what we perhaps misleadingly call the 'religious' wars of the period.

Within the context of a religiously divided Europe, René Descartes proposed to find something that could not under any circumstances be doubted, and rebuild a philosophical foundation on that basis. In his famous experiment of 1619, where he locked himself into a heated room, resolving not to come out until he found something he could not doubt, he finally emerged knowing that the fact that he doubted was what he was looking for. So a new epistemology appeared, based upon human self-consciousness and rationality. At the time, his younger followers exhibited boundless confidence that the puzzle of human certainty had been solved. Yet it was not long before questions arose. In the later Enlightenment, this confidence in reason was soon identified as hubris. Immanuel Kant's *Critique of Pure Reason*, published in 1781, directed as much against Hume's empiricism as Descartes' rationalism, pointed out the limits of confidence that elementary truths could be derived from sensory evidence or rational calculation: instead there were what he called 'synthetic' or *a priori* truths that must simply be assumed, rather than proved, much as the elementary propositions of mathematics. We can't easily prove that 2+2=4 – we just sense it to be the case. John Locke's empiricism proposed a different approach, focusing on our experience of life and nature as the course of our ideas about the world.

At the same time, a number of writers developed a similar critique of Enlightenment confidence in reason from a distinctively Christian perspective. In so doing they laid the foundations for the kind of epistemology that makes room for the importance of direct experience of God.

Blaise Pascal

Writing in the seventeenth century, Pascal wrote against the background of two very different intellectual movements of his time. On the one hand there were the followers of Descartes, thinkers who were very confident in the power of human rationality to discover truth. On the other hand, there were the followers of Montaigne, the sixteenth-century French moralist, whose main question was *'Que sais-je?'* What can I know for sure? His followers in Pascal's time were known by various names, *Pyrrhonistes* or *Libertins*, but the common denominator was a deep scepticism about our ability to know anything for certain.

In Pascal's own time, a type of Christian apologetics had arisen that saw rationalism as no great problem. This was because Christianity could be shown to be rational with the help of evidences from nature, Old Testament prophecy, miracles or logical arguments, and therefore prove its own truth. Pascal was less sure. In particular he raised three main arguments against both philosophical and theological rationalism. First he argued that human reason was not as reliable as its devotees thought. In fact the imagination is far more persuasive:

> Put the world's greatest philosopher on a plank that is wider than
> need be; if there is a precipice below, although his reason may
> convince him that he is safe, his imagination will prevail![5]

We believe what our feelings and passions tell us to believe, even if it is irrational. In other words, we believe what we want to believe. Desire is the hidden power that lies behind much of our pretence to objectivity. Thus, the heart is more significant than reason in coming to faith. For Pascal therefore, in perhaps his most famous saying: 'The heart has its reasons, of which Reason knows nothing.'[6]

Second, Pascal argued that the world is a deeply ambiguous place. Reason and the observation of nature do not necessarily lead to belief in God. The existence of suffering, disorder, pain, different religions, the often ambiguous nature of Scripture, even the concealment of God under the flesh of Jesus Christ mean that reason cannot compel faith. God's revelation is never obvious for us. On the other hand, there is enough suggestive evidence in miracles, Scripture and fulfilled prophecy to suggest there is more to life than just random irrationality. The world is so confusing and ambiguous, neither the rationalist nor the sceptic can fully explain it. Humankind is left dangling between arrogance and despair:

> That is what makes us incapable of certain knowledge or absolute
> ignorance. We are floating in a medium of vast extent, always
> uncertain and floating, blown from one place to another;

---

5. Pascal, B., *Pensées* (Harmondsworth: Penguin, 1966). This edition adopts the *Lafuma* numbering of the *Pensées*, usually denoted by the letter L. This fragment comes in L82.
6. *Ibid.*, L423.

whenever we think we have a fixed point to which we can cling
and make fast, it shifts and leaves us; if we follow it, it eludes
our grasp, slips away, and flees eternally before us. Nothing
stands still for us. This is our natural state and yet the state most
contrary to our inclinations. We burn with desire to find a firm
footing, an ultimate, steady base on which to build a tower rising
up to infinity, but our whole foundation cracks and the earth
opens up into the depths of the abyss.[7]

There is a profound hiddenness about God's self-revelation.
God hides the visible signs of his presence in the church and
the world 'in such a way that he will only be perceived by those
who seek him with all their heart.'[8]

Third, even if reason could lead to knowledge of God,
Pascal was concerned that it would lead to the wrong God, the
abstract impersonal God of the philosophers, not the living God
of Abraham, Isaac and Jacob. It would lead to a distant God,
not the living God who 'unites himself with (believers) in the
depths of their soul … and makes them incapable of having any
other end but him.' For Pascal, if there is to be any knowledge
of the true God, it must involve the heart and not just the
reason, because the true God engages us not just at the level of
intellect, but the whole person, beginning with the heart: 'it is
the heart that perceives God, and not the reason. That is what
faith is: God perceived by the heart, not by the reason.'[9]

The point is that for Pascal, there is no clear way to
God through pure reason. It can help, but not prove. It is
important to show that Christianity is not contrary to reason,
but something else is required to establish it in the heart: the
experience of God. Towards the end of his famous argument
of 'the wager' (which incidentally is not intended as a proof of
God's existence, but rather to show that the real reason many

---

7. *Ibid.*, L199.
8. *Ibid.*, L427, 155. This theme of hiddenness is also of course present in Jesus' own teaching – see Mt. 13.13.
9. *Ibid.*, L424, 154.

people don't believe is that they don't really want to), comes a
telling statement:

> If this discourse pleases you and seems impressive, know that it is
> made by a man who has knelt, both before and after it, in prayer
> to that Being, infinite and without parts, before whom he lays
> all he has, for you also to lay before Him all you have for your
> own good and for His glory, that so strength may be given to
> lowliness.[10]

This reflects Pascal's own experience in his 'Night of Fire' on 23
November 1654, when a dramatic experience of the presence
and reality of God dissolved his previous lukewarm faith and
formed the beginnings of a strong, passionate conviction. The
Mémorial, written presumably just afterwards, breathes the
language of fresh encounter with God:

> Certitude. Certitude. Feeling. Joy. Peace …
> Joy, joy, joy, tears of joy …
> Eternally in joy for a day's exercise on the earth.[11]

This led him to turn away from his previous shallow faith and
selfish materialism towards a new care for the poor of Paris and
a profound life of prayer and self-denial. It led him to a new
identity and a new vocation. For Pascal, this experience was
the key that unlocked the door of doubt and the ambiguity of
the world. Rationalism alone could not provide a way beyond
doubt into faith, or if it did, it left you with the dry arid God of
the philosophers. Pascal's epistemology, very conscious of the
new conditions of the early Enlightenment, leaves a vital place
for experience, the religion of the heart, a way to God unlocked
by a dramatic experience of the reality of God.

10. *Ibid.*, L418.
11. *Ibid.*, L913.

Jonathan Edwards

In the following century, another Christian philosopher, naturalist and theologian turned to consider similar issues but in a different context. Pascal was a Jansenist Roman Catholic, Jonathan Edwards a Puritan Protestant, yet the conclusions they came to are strikingly similar.

The revivals of the eighteenth century were themselves a kind of religious reaction to Enlightenment rationalism, just as Kantian metaphysics had been in the arena of ethical philosophy and Romanticism was in literature. Beginning with groups like the Moravians or *Herrnhuter* in eastern Europe, these revivals of Protestant faith spread westwards, finally reaching Britain with the conversions of George Whitefield and John Wesley in 1735 and 1738 respectively.[12] Jonathan Edwards was a contemporary of both of these, and was at the very heart of these movements both in Britain and America. More than perhaps any other theologian of the time, he was well aware that the pretensions to powerful manifestations of God visible in the 'Awakening' were a mixture of wishful thinking and genuine encounter. He also had to face the abiding Enlightenment distrust of emotion and preference for cool rationality, the spirit that made Joseph Butler utter his well-known rebuke to John Wesley: 'the pretending to extraordinary revelations and gifts of the Holy Ghost is a horrid thing, a very horrid thing!' Jonathan Edwards' work *The Religious Affections*, published in 1746, is a lengthy analysis of truth and falsehood in claims to religious experience, and of genuine and counterfeit signs of real encounter with God.

While acutely conscious of the possibility of spurious religious experience, Edwards is also one of the theologians most insistent that despite this tendency, the work of the Spirit is to be *felt*. New Testament conversions, he notes, are 'not wrought on in that silent, secret, gradual and insensible manner which is now insisted on; but with those manifest evidences

---

12. See Ward, W. R., *The Protestant Evangelical Awakening* (Cambridge: CUP, 1992) for an account of the eastern European origins of the Evangelical Awakening.

of a supernatural power wonderfully and suddenly causing a great change, which in these days are looked on as certain signs of delusion and enthusiasm.'[13] For Edwards, 'Without holy affection there is no true religion ... As there is no true religion where there is nothing else but affection, so there is no true religion where there is no religious affection.'[14]

His argument is that Scripture compares the work of God in the heart of people to such great acts of God as regeneration, new creation, and resurrection. He then asks a little mischievously:

> If it be indeed so ... that grace in the soul is so the effect of God's power, that it is fitly compared to those effects which are farthest from being owing to any strength in the subject, such as a generation, or a being begotten and resurrection, or a being raised from the dead, and creation, or a being brought out of nothing into being ... then what account can be given of it, that the Almighty, in so great a work of His power, should so carefully hide his power that the subjects of it should be able to discern nothing of it?[15]

The language is quaint, but the question spot on: if God's work in human hearts can be placed in the same category as creation or resurrection, wouldn't it be a little odd if we should feel nothing when God acts upon us? What follows is a lengthy and sophisticated analysis of the true signs of genuine spiritual life and experience as against the spurious. For him, the 'witness of the Spirit' does not give any new knowledge unavailable in scriptural revelation, but it is God's 'vital indwelling in the heart, exerting and communicating himself there in his own proper, holy or divine nature.'[16] Essentially, the mark of a genuine experience of the reality of God is the turning of an impersonal knowledge about God into a deeply personal love for him. The believer finds that she has an appetite for God,

13. Edwards, J., *The Religious Affections* (Edinburgh: Banner of Truth, 1986), 67.
14. *Ibid.*, 48–49.
15. *Ibid.*, 66f.
16. *Ibid.*, 164.

a 'certain divine spiritual taste' that was not there before. In a
sense, Edwards' argument is an aesthetic one: faith brings about
an ability to see beauty in God, to find him pleasing, desirable
and rather than distant or fearful (or non-existent!). Edwards
knows that a *love* for God cannot be generated by reason or by
moral effort: it is a work of the Spirit.

A comparison between Jonathan Edwards and Friedrich
Schleiermacher, another theologian whose thought focused on
feeling and experience, sharpens the point.[17] Kant's insistence
that we cannot know things-in-themselves, but only the
impression left on our minds by our perception of things,
had led to an erosion of confidence in any human ability to
access God objectively. We can only be sure of our subjective
impression of God, not God in himself. Locke's argument
that all our ideas come through our immediate senses also
disallowed any possibility of divine revelation that did not
just confirm what our senses told us anyway. Schleiermacher,
profoundly aware of these attacks on the possibility of direct
experience of God, proposed that religious experience is not
really experience of God at all – it is just a particular way of
looking at the world. For Schleiermacher, everyone experiences
a 'feeling of absolute dependence'. However, only some people
interpret that as 'God-consciousness'. In other words, the
experience is universal – you do not need any special capacity
to know the basic impression of dependence on something
outside yourself – you only need to begin to understand that
experience differently. What makes this experience religious is
not the experience itself, but the way in which you interpret it.

For Edwards, however, the 'spiritual sense' comes as a new
form of perception. Like Schleiermacher, Edwards agrees that
both believers and unbelievers have notions of God. However,
believers are given the ability to grasp the 'divine excellency'.
This 'glory', 'holiness', or 'beauty' of God is moreover an
objective quality of God, only accessible to the saints by the
light of grace. It is not just a different way of looking at things,

---

17. This section draws on a very helpful discussion in McClymond, M., *Encounters with God: An Approach to the Theology of Jonathan Edwards* (New York: OUP, 1998), 22–24.

a different interpretation of an experience accessible to all, as Schleiermacher said.[18] The believer does experience something different from the unbeliever – the beauty and holiness of God – and this is not just a subjective experience, but an apprehension of an objective reality.

The question remains then, how you can discern true experience of God from false? In *The Religious Affections*, Edwards continues to recount a list of factors that characterise true religious experience. One of these concerns the 'certainty' of faith. For him, it is true affections that alone can bring about a confident, robust faith. Reason cannot perform that miracle.

> All those who are truly gracious persons have a solid, full, thorough and effectual conviction of the truth of the great things of the gospel; I mean, that they no longer halt between two opinions; the great doctrines of the gospel cease to be any longer doubtful things, or matters of opinion, which, though probable, are yet disputable; but with them, they are points settled and determined, as undoubted and indisputable, so that they are not afraid to venture their all upon their truth.[19]

True affections bring about a kind of certainty that is not mathematical or logical in nature. It is a curious symptom of our culture that we assume that if we cannot find logical or scientific certainty, then we must surrender to a shrug of the shoulders, a relativistic reticence about truth or conviction. Edwards, however, points out an alternative that depends on the true nature of Christian certainty. For him, this certainty is not dependent upon a watertight argument or proof for the existence of God. True Christian experience, or 'religious affection' as Edwards describes it, brings about a different

---

18. 'Edwards clearly would not have accepted Schleiermacher's notion of an implicit awareness of God, that is, a state in which the subject does not recognise God as the object of his or her experience. The mark of genuine spiritual perception is seeing the very "divinity" of God. What also decisively separated Edwards from Schleiermacher and the Romantics generally, was his sharp distinction between the mentality of the regenerate and the unregenerate. For Schleiermacher, the capacity for religious feeling was an intrinsic aspect of human nature per se, and not a special gift that God confers on selected individuals.', 23f.
19. *Ibid.*, 217.

kind of certainty – the certainty of the heart, that is more about personal conviction, an utter trust in a person rather than being convinced by an argument. Such conviction does include and involve rational thought but it is not confined to it alone: 'it is requisite not only that the belief which their affections arise from, should be a reasonable, but also a spiritual belief or conviction.'[20] Such spiritual conviction is an ability to see things in their true nature, and is a gift of the Spirit, not natural reason. It comes about due to 'the Spirit of God's enlightening the mind, to have right apprehensions of the nature of those things, and so as it were unveiling things, or revealing them, and enabling the mind to view them and see them as they are.'[21]

In particular it is only such conviction that can lead to true, self-abandoning discipleship. Rational argument can take you so far, but ultimately only this kind of spiritual perception, coming through the gift of the Spirit rather than rational argumentation, can enable a person to live a life of joyful self-denial and service:

> But to have a conviction, so clear, and evident, and assuring, as to be sufficient to induce them, with boldness to sell all, confidently and fearlessly to run the venture of the loss of all things, and of enduring the most exquisite and long continued torments, and to trample the world under foot, and count all things but dung for Christ, the evidence they can have from history, cannot be sufficient.[22]

For Edwards, knowledge of Christian truth, identity or vocation is not dependent upon the whims or fashions of scholarship. If it were, it would be a very aristocratic thing whereby only the best of scholars had access to conviction and truth. The gift of the Spirit does not counter reason, but removes intellectual objections to faith and helps reason see truth and beauty where before it could not do so. In an apologetic context, evidence

20. Edwards, *The Religious Affections*, 221.
21. *Ibid.*, 222.
22. *Ibid.*, 229.

might be presented – evidence for the historicity of Jesus, or the resurrection. However, these are penultimate not ultimate. As Edwards puts it:

> Though great use may be made of external arguments, they are not to be neglected, but highly prized and valued; for they may be greatly serviceable to awaken unbelievers, and bring them to serious consideration, and to confirm the faith of true saints; yea, they may be in some respect subservient to the begetting of a saving faith in men.

At the end of the day, such arguments are preparatory for what really needs to take place: a kind of spiritual illumination that lifts these evidences into the realm of conviction. The disciples on the road to Emmaus in the story recounted in Luke 24 walk with Jesus and hear his teaching, yet are blind to what is really happening until their eyes are opened. It is only at that point that the penny drops, and real spiritual understanding dawns.

Edwards' account is a useful exploration of the relationships between reason and faith, evidence and inspiration, argument and experience. The experience of the Spirit does not contradict reason, but takes it where it cannot go unaided, into the region of a spiritual certainty. Faith for him is not opposed to reason, it is in fact a form of knowledge that is different from and yet complementary to reason. Yet this certainty, because it is not founded on logical argumentation, leaves room for intellectual exploration, even doubt. Because it is a kind of aesthetic conviction of the beauty and goodness of God, or a personal confidence in the trustworthiness of God, it enables rather than closes down intellectual discovery and theological enquiry. It is the certainty of faith first and foremost, and therefore it is open to questions and a level of uncertainty when it comes to precise theological formulations of doctrine. It is a different form of certainty from a rigid, unquestionable fixity of mind. Instead it opens up the mind to the exploration of what has been encountered through the Spirit.

Alvin Plantinga

Taking a leap into more recent times, the Christian philosopher
Alvin Plantinga takes this line of argument further. He asks
the basic question of Christian epistemology: how do believers
know that what they believe is true? His answer is that
Christian belief arises not by inference or argument, but comes
about in a more instinctive way. We have a sense of the divine,
a *sensus divinitatis*, but this has been weakened by sin to the
extent that it is unreliable and inexact, and its malfunctioning
often results in a lack of belief in God. This innate divine sense
needs renewing and healing, and this is performed by the
Holy Spirit. In a model derived from both Thomas Aquinas
and John Calvin (an unlikely pairing that reaffirms this as
being a centrally Christian set of insights, not simply confined
to one part of the universal church) he argues that faith is not
established by some external compelling argument but, for the
believer, it just *seems* to be true in an 'intuitive and immediate'
way. It is the same with the elementary truths of mathematics or
memory: they are assumed to be true, not because of some prior
argument or proof, but because they just seem to make sense.
As with Jonathan Edwards, faith is not opposed to knowledge,
but it is a different kind of knowledge from that available
through argumentation and reason: 'Those who have faith have
a source of knowledge that transcends our ordinary perceptual
faculties and cognitive processes …'[23] As Thomas Aquinas
says: 'The Holy Spirit makes us lovers of God'. And as we have
already seen, Calvin's theology of the Spirit makes a claim to
objective and not just subjective knowledge of God. Echoing
Edwards, Plantinga argues that Christian faith is a matter of
true affections. The difference between devils and saints is not
what they believe (both believe in the existence of God!)[24] but
in their feelings towards what they believe in.[25] Devils believe
in God but are filled with loathing for him. Saints believe

23. Plantinga, A., *Warranted Christian Belief* (New York: OUP, 2000), 266.
24. Jas. 2.19.
25. Plantinga, *Warranted Christian Belief*, 293.

in God and are filled with joy and delight at the thought. Such affections or feelings about God cannot be produced by argument or inference – they arise in a much more basic way.

Plantinga's 'reformed epistemology' is much too complex to be examined in detail here. His main point for our purposes, however, is that belief in God is brought about not primarily by argumentation, but by a range of possible factors that incline someone to believe, and that logically, this is enough. The believer does not need to present arguments to support it: it is in Plantinga's words, 'properly basic'. The proper stages of this belief are the statements of Scripture, the presence and action of the Holy Spirit, and the gift of faith, which as we have already seen in Calvin is the principal gift of the Spirit.[26] This approach, like those of Pascal and Edwards, suggests that faith comes about through the mysterious work of the Spirit, through the opening up of the heart and the mind to experience of a new dimension of reality that generates a new love for God, which cannot come about in any other way.

Philip Toynbee

Philip Toynbee was a communist, writer, journalist, depressive and father of the now stridently atheist Polly Toynbee. Coming to a tentative faith in God late in life, he wrote a small book, which has become something of a classic, called *Towards the Holy Spirit: A Tract for the Times*. Though he is impatient with many aspects of traditional Christian theology, he still senses that much of reality is simply inconceivable to the human mind. For him, it is the mystics, those who experience a reality beyond the visible or rational, who hold the key.

> As for the mystics – and these are far and away the most coherent and impressive body of witnesses – not one of them has ever accepted that his experience *could have been* either hallucinatory or compensatory. Indeed what they tell us is that the reality they

---

26. *Ibid.*, 243f.

have been made aware of during their visionary states is infinitely more real than the reality of everyday living. It is true of course that people often misinterpret their own experiences. *But the experiencers are always the primal witnesses* and their testament is of immeasurably greater value, *a priori*, than any interpretation which others may choose to put on it.[27]

Toynbee's is a very different kind of approach to the more theologically focused arguments found in Pascal, Edwards and Plantinga, yet his *cri de coeur* makes an important point: the validity and perhaps even unanswerability of experience of a reality beyond the ordinary. To the one who experiences something of this kind, it is real. The fact that it cannot be communicated in words does not gainsay it – it carries its own conviction. For him, 'the final end/purpose/endeavour of the Holy Spirit is to spiritualise the whole of the phenomenal universe',[28] echoing the idea in John's Gospel that the Spirit gives life (Jn. 6.63) and the Pauline idea that the Spirit is a foretaste of the new creation. He sees the Spirit as overseeing or pulling the world to its evolutionary end. Toynbee concludes his thoughts with this claim:

> It does not seem irrational, superstitious or beyond our means, to speak of the Holy Spirit and to pray for the Spirit's descent upon ourselves and on our world … But far more important than any phrase or formulation, however rich in association and restored significance, is the capacity to wait in a state of attention, cultivating the attentive faculties of love, hope and faith …[29]

Experience, Faith and the Ancient Gift of Tongues

Toynbee argued that the one thing needed in a fractured yet evolving world is to pray for the descent of the Holy Spirit. For people to discover this new identity and vocation, for us

---

27. Toynbee, P., *Towards the Holy Spirit* (London: SCM, 1973), 49f. Italics his
28. *Ibid.*, 70.
29. *Ibid.*, 73.

to find out who we are and what we are here for, requires the action of the Holy Spirit. It is only when the Spirit brings us into union with Christ so that we know the love of the Father and find ourselves sent back into the world, that these notions turn from ideas into experience. The prayer of invocation of the Holy Spirit is therefore a prayer for a new identity and vocation. It asks the Spirit to unite us with Christ so we know the love of the Father. It cries out for the completion of creation, and that we will find our lives transfigured and transformed into what they have the God-given potential to become: beloved children of God, called to work with him for the renewal of creation.

It is a prayer for faith. If faith is a gift of the Spirit, this is at the heart of the prayer for the Holy Spirit. It is the prayer to turn knowledge into love, to generate an appetite for God, as we saw in the theology of Jonathan Edwards. It is also a prayer that expects an answer. It expects that when we pray 'Come Holy Spirit' the answer to that prayer will be the beginning of a real experience of the love of God in Christ, evoking and giving birth to faith, and as we saw in a previous chapter, being drawn into compassion and suffering for the sake of the world. Exactly what is experienced at the moment of invocation of the Spirit will vary from person to person. In fact it may be best to understand the reactions that various people have when such a prayer is prayed not so much as the Spirit directly dictating the way they react, as if God chooses to make one person weep, another laugh, another feel a strong shiver of emotion through their body, another experience a quiet sense of well-being. Instead, our different personalities and experiences react in different ways to the same Spirit. As the Roman Catholic theologian Simon Tugwell puts it:

> The working of the Holy Spirit may not always conform to our ideas of propriety. If he really gets down to spring-cleaning the depths of our soul, some pretty unsavoury specimens are likely to be produced! The Spirit works on our nature, as it actually is, and that includes any hang-ups, blockages, obsessions and so on that

we happen to have ... we must never expect any manifestation
of 'neat Holy Spirit'; there will always be an element of our own
human spirit in any genuine manifestation of the Holy Spirit.[30]

Dramatic experiences that occur in answer to this prayer are of
course much more common in Christian history than we might
suppose. A cool, rationalistic, reserved faith is really a post-
Enlightenment phenomenon, not necessarily typical of faith as
it manifests itself across the traditions and centuries of Christian
experience. To take a couple of examples, the fourteenth-
century Gregory of Sinai wrote a work not dissimilar to that of
Jonathan Edwards on the nature and effects of the Spirit's work
in people from within the Greek Orthodox monastic tradition
of Mount Athos, trying to discern the true signs of the Spirit
working from false:

There are several signs that the energy of the Holy Spirit is
beginning to be active in those who genuinely aspire for this
to happen ... In some it appears as awe arising in the heart,
in others as a tremulous sense of jubilation, in others as joy, in
others as joy mingled with awe, or as trembling mingled with joy
and sometimes it manifests itself as tears and awe.[31]

St Isaac the Syrian, the seventh-century mystical theologian,
writes of the Spirit's gift of tears:

And when the time for the birth has arrived, the intellect begins
to sense something of the things of that other world – as a faint
perfume, or as the breath of life which a newborn child receives
into its bodily frame. But we are not accustomed to such an
experience and, finding it hard to endure, our body is suddenly
overcome by a weeping mingled with joy.[32]

The gift of tongues has often been seen as a tangible sign of

---

30. Tugwell, S., *Did You Receive the Spirit?* (London: Darton, Longman & Todd, 1972), 68.
31. Palmer, G. E. H.; Sherrard, P.; et al. (eds.), *The Philokalia: The Complete Text, compiled by St
Nikodemos of the Holy Mountain and St Makarios of Corinth* (London: Faber & Faber, 1995), 259.
32. Quoted in Ware, K., *The Orthodox Way* (New York: St Vladimir's Seminary Press, 1979), 101.

the Spirit's presence, and can be seen as playing a potentially significant role at the start of a person's Christian faith. Philip Toynbee again has an intriguing insight into this. In speaking of the realm of spiritual experience and encounter with God, human language struggles to cope:

> ... the language we have to use in this near-inexpressible area of human experience is at the very opposite extreme from that which used to be demanded by the positivist philosophers ... It is a ghostly language, a language of hint and suggestion, of echo and paradox: something much closer to the untranslatable communications of music than to the demonstrations of logic.[33]

A 'language at the opposite end of positivistic philosophy' sounds not far from the structured but unintelligible language of the ancient Christian gift of tongues. Again this is nothing new. St Paul himself spoke in tongues. St Augustine describes the kind of prayer known as *Jubilatio*, where people praise God in random syllables because the voice cannot express the joy of the heart. Until the ninth century, this practice of *Jubilatio* became formalised in the Orthodox liturgy as the congregation would improvise with the 'A' sound at the end of the 'Alleluia'. St Teresa of Avila and John of the Cross both testify to praising God in singing with sounds that are not so much words as an expression of spiritual joy.

It is easy to miss the significance of this by concentrating on its exotic and unusual character. All of the writers we have considered in this chapter insist that faith is a gift of the Spirit, not produced by inference or rational means, yet not in itself irrational. Instead, faith introduces us to a new certainty, a new rationality. Jean-Jacques Suurmond suggests that ecstatic gifts such as tongues help to break through the excessive control of the analytical intellect and to make us open to an encounter with God in the deeper levels of our being.'[34] Perhaps the gift

33. Toynbee, *Towards the Holy Spirit*, 63.
34. Suurmond, J.-J., *Word and Spirit at Play: Towards a Charismatic Theology* (Grand Rapids: Eerdmans, 1995), 79.

of tongues acts as a kind of gateway into this new rationality of the Spirit, the kingdom of God, which operates according to different rules from the normal ones that govern 'ordinary life'. Tongues has sometimes been called a 'love language' and can be seen as a way of responding to a deep experience of the love of God in a new language that starts where normal human language stops, that expresses a reaction to love when normal analytical human language just seems inadequate. Of course not every Christian speaks in tongues, yet the gift can serve as a form of surrender, a willingness to let go of control, and begin the path of conformity to the will and purpose of God. Echoing the teaching of St Isaac the Syrian, Bishop Kallistos Ware from the Orthodox Christian tradition writes:

> When it is genuinely spiritual, 'speaking with tongues' seems to represent an act of 'letting go' – the crucial moment in the breaking down of our sinful self-trust, and its replacement by a willingness to allow God to act within us. In the Orthodox tradition, this act of 'letting go' more often takes the form of the gift of tears.[35]

The gift of tongues can be a kind of release, a willingness to go beyond the rational control of the mind, to begin the process of self-surrender to God. Simon Tugwell comments: 'You cannot pray in tongues unless you are prepared to make a fool of yourself, and let something happen to you, over which your mind has none of its usual control. You cannot engineer tongues, any more than you could engineer the kind of weeping that Isaac or Symeon was talking about, or St Teresa's prayer of quiet.'[36] For Michael Welker, the gift of tongues offers a centre around which a countermovement to the church's tendency to 'liturgical ossification, theological abstraction ... and forms of moralism'[37] can develop.

Other 'spiritual gifts' can be seen in this light too. If the

---

35. Ware, *The Orthodox Way*, 101.
36. Tugwell, *Did you Receive the Spirit?*, 63 37. Welker, M. *God the Spirit* (Minneapolis: Fortress, 1994), 268f..
37. Welker, M., *God the Spirit* (Minneapolis: Fortress, 1994), 268f.

work of the prodigal Spirit is to reach into the far country to draw us back into the love of God between Father and Son, then perhaps the gift of prophecy might be seen as the ability to see the world, or the person to whom it is given, as beloved. A prophetic word either foresees the future or places the person or situation it refers to in a different light. It can see a new reality because it imagines that person or community embraced in the healing and restoring love of God, which might be a very different place to where they are at the time.

The Place of Experience and the Prodigal Spirit

The Trinitarian theology we explored in chapter one spoke of the heart of reality being the love between the Father and the Son. The Spirit unites us with Christ so that we begin to experience the same depth of love that exists between the Father and the Son. We feel the embrace of the Father and the returning love of the Son arising in our own hearts. Pascal, Edwards and Plantinga all write of the importance of the possibility of experience of the love of God as the fundamental difference between a sterile, formal faith and one that is alive and real.

If the Spirit brings us into the lived experience of the love that is at the heart of God – the love between Father and Son – then there is inevitably an experiential dimension to the work of the Spirit. Whereas before there might have been little love for God, little love for the neighbour, let alone the enemy, when the Spirit comes, he brings about a love for God and a love for the rest of creation. This experience of love is not an appreciation of the benefits of mutual cooperation or a doctrinal grasp of the theology of the Trinity – it is an actual sharing in the love that exists in the heart of God.

In many churches, when the invocation of the Spirit is made, people are encouraged to stand with hands held out, palms open, as a kind of liturgical sign of openness to receive.

Sometimes something tangible is received, a distinct experience of love, joy, power, grace. Sometimes very little is actually felt. Yet there is something very significant in that gesture. It is something the Catholic Christian tradition strives after in its focus on Mary, the mother of Jesus. Her simple prayer, 'I am the Lord's servant; may it be to me as you have said' (Lk. 1.38) is one of the Bible's greatest expressions of receptivity, of a simple willingness to be at God's disposal, to lay aside all personal ambitions and plans. Philip Toynbee again expresses it well: 'the supreme function of men and women is to receive God's gifts, the light of heaven, as fully as they can ...'[38] That is the most basic and best stance of any human being, not imposing, not demanding, but waiting for God's gifts, being ready to be filled with God's Spirit who brings out our full potential and alone enables us to do God's work in the world.

Whether or not something is experienced at that moment is perhaps more important at the start of Christian faith than later on. An experience of the Spirit such as that which many tentative believers or sceptical agnostics receive in the early stages of faith is a powerful confirmation of the reality of God, a moment when the idea of God that might have been discussed at length no longer seems a mere idea, but becomes a person, full of intent and love. The repeating of this gesture, however, week after week in the liturgical practice of the church is a powerful statement of the basic human stance towards God. We do not offer God our gifts, abilities, status or money as if we are doing him a favour. We wait for him, expectant and patient, standing silently in awe of him, waiting for the gift of his Spirit who gives new identity and a new calling.

This experience is not a random spiritual high, a religious equivalent of the addict's fix, a shot of high-octane religion, but is the beginnings of a sharing in the love between the Father and the Son. It is the beginnings of desire for what is truly good, beautiful and true. In a sense it is theologically a little inaccurate to call it the 'experience of the Spirit' – more properly it is the experience of the love between the Father and the Son, through

---

38. Toynbee, *Towards the Holy Spirit*, 83.

the Spirit. Or to put it in different, more eschatological terms, it is an experience of the future, the resurrection, the Spirit as a downpayment of the age to come. This instantly takes it out of the limited realm of 'charismatic' Christianity, or mystical elitism, into the inheritance of all Christians. The vital thing is not the particular tradition in which it is expressed, but the reality of the experience itself, and the theological framework in which it is understood.

The Dramatic and the Ordinary

Having said all this, one further point needs to be made. There is a particular tendency for churches and individuals who emphasise the immediate experience of God to become alarmingly dualist, with great attention being paid to miraculous healings or spiritual experiences and less fuss made of the more ordinary, mundane aspects of life. In reaction to forms of Christian faith that deny the possibility of the miraculous, it is tempting to adopt a form of Christian life that sees God in the supernatural but not the natural, the dramatic but not the ordinary. This is effectively to deny the goodness of creation as an arena of God's presence and action, and introduces a semi-gnostic, spiritualising tendency that limits God to the ecstatic experience and misses him in more normal encounters and experiences.

People who have been deeply affected by a profound encounter with God often remark on how the world suddenly seems bigger. There are new possibilities, horizons expand, and the world seems full of colour, space and potential. It is as if the world suddenly gets larger; as if a new dimension of reality has opened up. This language of dimensions might help at this point. We are aware of three dimensions of space, but can perhaps imagine the discovery of an extra fourth dimension, an idea that has fascinated mathematicians and physicists since the nineteenth century, and often, since Einstein, linked to the idea of time. The three spatial dimensions we know of through immediate experience all intersect with each other so that they are not distinct entities. However, if you take away one of them, our experience of reality while not impossible, would be very different. A fourth dimension would presumably likewise bring about a whole new way of looking at the world, while at the same time not doing away with the three dimensions we know of already.

It might be useful to think of human life as lived in a number of intersecting dimensions, such as the physical, the intellectual and the social. 'Life in the Spirit' then might be conceived as more like an extra dimension to life that complements and informs the other dimensions, rather than being an alternative to them. Life in the Spirit, an awareness of and openness to the reality of God, the miraculous and the spiritual, is not so much an alternative mode of reality, or one that cancels out the others, as one that adds to and enriches them, in the same way that depth adds to and enriches our perception of height and length. To over-emphasise the supernatural or the miraculous, or to deny the natural or the ordinary as a vehicle for the presence and action of God would be like suggesting that depth is so important and wonderful that we no longer need height or length. At the same time, ignoring or denying depth is to try to live in a diminished universe, a two-dimensional world. To deny the reality of direct divine action, the experience of God through the Spirit or the possibility of the miraculous is also to live in a diminished universe, one that quite simply misses a vital area of life and reality.[39]

This kind of approach establishes a proper relationship between life in the Spirit and the more 'natural' dimensions of the physical, intellectual and the social. It is not that God is only at work in the dramatic and the 'supernatural', yet neither need we deny the importance of this dimension of reality. To see life in the Spirit as an extra dimension of our experience enables a properly holistic vision of the spiritual life that is not opposed to the physical, the intellectual or the social, but

---

39. Michael Welker writes of the Spirit as creating a 'force-field'; Welker, God the Spirit, 235f.

embraces, enhances and adds depth to them. It overcomes any tendency towards an unhelpful dualism and replaces it with a richer view of reality. It implies that the fullness of the spiritual life will be open to and require development, growth and expression in all of these dimensions. A truly spiritual person will be someone with developed maturity in the intellectual sphere, in engagement with their physical environment, in social and interpersonal relationships and also in experience and encounter with God. Being filled with the Spirit completes a person, so that they finally discover their true identity and calling: being in Christ and becoming like Christ.

The church is the community that bears witness to and embodies the life of the kingdom of God, the realm in which the love of God heals and transforms. If it is to do that, it will need the presence of the Spirit who is the one who gives a foretaste of that kingdom, inaugurated by the life, death and resurrection of Jesus Christ – the new creation. At the same time, the role of the Spirit is to draw us into the love between the Father and the Son, an action that assumes the importance and possibility of actual experience of that love, an experience that so often unlocks the door to a new confidence in who we are – loved by the Father in Christ – and a new purpose in life, healing and caring for the creation. Such an experience is however only the start. It is a gateway. To hanker after such experience at all times is a sign of immaturity, yet to assume that the Christian has to live henceforth on a diet of spiritual memory and nostalgia is to miss the significance of the relationship into which it initiates us. The ministry of the prodigal Spirit is not a once and for all movement, it is a constant rhythm of the Christian life.

CHAPTER 4

THE HOLY SPIRIT AND CHARACTER

Experience of God may be possible. But something more than momentary experience is needed if a new identity is to be found and our calling fulfilled. And that is the transformation of a momentary experience of the love and power of God into a lifelong change of settled character and patterns of behaviour.

One of the best known explorations of the work of the Holy Spirit in the New Testament is in Galatians, where Paul speaks of the fruit of the Spirit. In chapter 5, during a discussion describing Christian life as 'walking by the Spirit', he recounts a list of Christian characteristics that bears close relationship to similar lists of virtues which appear in contemporary pagan writings. However, in this case he doesn't use the normal Greek word for virtue (*aretē*) but instead he calls them 'fruit of the Spirit'. The word is in the singular, indicating that they possess an essential unity – this is the quality of life that tends to emerge in a human life when the Holy Spirit is present and active. It is what Catholic writers sometimes called habitual grace, and Protestant theologians eventually called the work of sanctification, or making holy. It refers to the Spirit's work in the gradual transformation of character.

Character, of course, is different from personality. Personality might be described as the distinguishing marks of an individual that are morally neutral, such as whether they are extrovert or introvert, thoughtful or spontaneous, dynamic or quiet. It is not particularly admirable to be either one or the other of any of these. Character is something different. It describes characteristics that do have moral weight: whether someone is courageous or cowardly, gentle or harsh, patient or impatient. Moreover, character describes a pattern of behaviour, a deep, structural tendency towards these actions. A person of true character is someone who more often than not acts generously, kindly, courageously or patiently. It is not someone who might occasionally perform an act of generosity or self-control, but someone in whom these things are natural, almost normal. As Dallas Willard puts it: 'Our character is that internal, overall structure of the self that is revealed by our long-term patterns of behaviour, and from which our actions more or less automatically arise.'[1]

By chance, a complete novice might just run their fingers over a piano keyboard and play a decent-sounding tune, but it's unlikely. A beginner might learn how to play one tune and do it fairly well, but is lost when it comes to other more complex pieces. A concert pianist can play more or less anything she wants to: whether sight-reading, or playing by ear, or playing a complex piece by memory. A good pianist is one who by constant training and practice has come to the point where they play wonderfully-sounding music on the piano almost without thinking about it. The novice has to think about every note. For an expert, it comes naturally, by second nature. And of course, no one just plays the piano – it has to be learnt, as does any skill such as making chairs, shoes, legal documents or playing tennis.

This is what virtue is: a quality of life that enables you to perform a difficult task easily and often. Josef Pieper writes: 'real perfected virtue by the very nature of its concept, bears the joyous, radiant seal of ease, of effortlessness, of self-evident

1. Willard, D., *Renovation of the Heart: Putting on the Character of Christ* (Colorado Springs: NavPress, 2002), 142.

inclination.'[2] The question for us is: how does Christian virtue come about?

The Origins of Virtue

The piano illustration would suggest that it comes about by practice. Do one thing often enough and it becomes a habit. Good character is the result of long habits of life. For most of us, brushing your teeth at night is not something you have to remember to do by setting your alarm, or leaving post-it notes on the bathroom door to make sure you remember. It is something you just do before you go to bed because you have always done it.

This is basically the Aristotelian approach to virtue. Aristotle believed that virtue is acquired by practice: 'Anything that we have to learn to do, we learn by the actual doing of it. People become builders by building and instrumentalists by playing instruments. Similarly we become just by performing just acts, temperate by performing temperate ones, brave by performing brave ones.'[3] Being good comes from doing good. If you force yourself to give money away, even if at first it feels odd and counter-intuitive, and you keep doing it, eventually it becomes natural, and straightforward. You become a generous person.

Medieval theologians like Thomas Aquinas adapted and developed this idea in distinctively Christian ways in their moral theology, blending it with Augustine's idea of co-operative grace, whereby grace enables us to co-operate with God to produce Christ-like character.[4] In this scheme, Christian character is the result of both the work of the Holy Spirit (often in fact virtually synonymous with 'grace' in medieval theology) and human effort and action.

2. Pieper, J., *The Four Cardinal Virtues* (Notre Dame: University of Notre Dame Press, 1990), 163.
3. Aristotle (Tredennick. H, trans.), *The Nicomachean Ethics* (London: Penguin, 1953), 1130a.33–37.
4. For example, for Aquinas, habitual actions enhance rather than create character, as Aristotle would have said: 'Acts produced by an infused habit do not cause a habit, but strengthen the already existing habit; just as the remedies of medicine given to a man who is naturally healthy, do not cause a kind of health, but give new strength to the health he had before.' *Summa Theologica*, 1a2æ.51.4.

Reformation writers, however, were deeply suspicious of this approach. Luther in particular felt that advising people to do good works so that in time they would become good was a recipe for hypocrisy, pride and self-delusion. It led to hypocrisy because it made you act in a false way, performing outward acts that were not reflected in the heart, and which led to a disjunction between visible outward action and hidden inner motivation: acting kindly with a smile that hid a heart full of malice. It led to pride because even if it did produce a habit of kindness, it was your own achievement, leading not to dependence on God but self-reliance, and the intolerable smugness of the 'self-made man' who is good and knows it. Finally it led to self-delusion because it made you think you were fine, good and acceptable before God whereas no one was ever meant to be justified before God on the basis of human virtue. We were always meant to be justified through faith, or perhaps better, through a fundamental attitude of trust towards God, rather than trying to make ourselves good enough for him. For Luther the starting point in coming to know God is not an instruction to try harder, but the good news that in Christ God has come near to us, and provided in Christ the righteousness we need. All we are asked to do is to believe that is true, and be grateful. Transformation of life and behaviour does flow from that realisation, leading to a very different way of life and pattern of behaviour, but it is vital not to confuse categories: works matter but they do not justify; only faith does.[5]

For Luther therefore, goodness comes about through the act of faith, which is itself a gift of the Holy Spirit. He believed that good action came about almost automatically, as a result of having grasped this astounding news that we are justified, made right with God, freely by grace through faith, and not by repeated works that build up habits of grace, as most medieval theologians taught.

5. I have discussed Luther's thought on virtue in Chapter 6 of Tomlin, G., *Spiritual Fitness: Christian Character in a Consumer Culture* (London: Continuum, 2006).

Virtue is therefore something of a contested notion in Christian theology. It is more at home in Catholic than Protestant theology (Karl Barth also had his doubts about it), and there are things to be said on both sides of this debate. Put crudely, Catholic versions of virtue teaching can tend at times to make God's love seem conditional upon our progress in goodness, leading to a rather strenuous and anxious spirituality. Protestant reactions, on the other hand, could lead to the presumption that because only faith justifies, only faith matters. No effort or discipline is needed in the Christian life and growth into Christ-likeness of character is an optional extra. Nice if you can do it, but not strictly necessary for salvation and therefore marginal.

In terms of the theology of the Spirit, Luther represents one strand of Christian teaching that emphasises the suddenness of change, the priority of the Holy Spirit as the one who produces goodness in us without our help. Aquinas, following Aristotle, represents the other Christian tradition that emphasises the way in which we are to work hard at our moral transformation, co-operating with God in the building of character.

So how are we to understand this? Given what we have considered so far, how is the experience of God's work through the Holy Spirit explored in the last chapters, related to the long-term, steady development of these qualities of life, these virtues designated the 'fruit of the Spirit'? Is transformation of life the result of direct experiences of the Spirit, or the result of a regime of spiritual disciplines that build up moral fibre, just as physical exercise builds up bodily strength? What is the relationship between the experience of the presence and power of God and the acquisition of a settled, steady Christian character of life? Is Christ-like character the work of the Spirit or the work of human effort? If both are involved, how do they relate to one another? In short, how does the Spirit change us?

The Holy Spirit and Christian Character in the Bible

John Levison's book *Filled with the Spirit* explores the various strands of teaching on the Holy Spirit in the Bible.[6] For him, generally speaking, the Old Testament sees no great distinction between the divine Spirit and the spirit breathed into human bodies to give them life and energy. To be 'filled with the Spirit' in the Old Testament meant to be filled to the *nth* degree with life or excellence. It could describe an extraordinary level of skill or intelligence, a difference in intensity of 'life' and the human spirit, rather than the addition of an extra, external power from beyond. It is also something that is built up over a period of time, through the natural acquisition of expertise, skill and experience. Bezalel, for example is 'filled … with the Spirit of God, with skill, ability and knowledge in all kinds of crafts – to make artistic designs for work in gold, silver and bronze, to cut and set stones, to work in wood, and to engage in all kinds of craftsmanship' (Ex. 31.3–5). This filling with the Spirit is entirely compatible with a skill acquired over years of learning, training and formation. Joshua is filled with the Spirit of Wisdom (Dt. 34.9) and this wisdom is clearly a quality acquired both through a lifetime of experience and through the laying on of Moses' hands.

The New Testament has something of this. John the Baptist 'grew and became strong in spirit' (Lk. 1.80), and Stephen is 'a man full of faith and the Holy Spirit' (Acts 6.5). However, at least in part under the influence, as Levison suggests, of the fascination for the ecstatic in first-century Graeco-Roman religion and culture, the early Christians saw the Holy Spirit as an extra gift coming on the heels of faith in Christ: 'an additional endowment that is other, or more, than the God-given spirit of birth.'[7] However, going beyond the Greek interest in the ecstatic, early Christian understandings of the Spirit combined both rapture and rationality. The unique quality of the account of the day of Pentecost in the book of Acts is

6. Levison, J. R., *Filled with the Spirit* (Grand Rapids: Eerdmans, 2009).
7. *Ibid.*, 423.

the blend of ecstatic experience and intelligibility: the gift of tongues experienced on that day was both something beyond the rational and expected but also enabled people of different languages and cultures to hear the good news intelligibly in their own tongue.

In the Pauline letters, being 'filled with the Spirit' tends to mean a numinous experience that leads to powers beyond the normal or natural. It is placed in parallel to drunkenness as a form of ecstasy (Eph. 5.18), and signs and miracles are performed by the power of the Spirit (Rom. 15.19). Luke has a variety of emphases. On the one hand, the Spirit inspires prophetic words (Lk. 1.67), enables the supernatural gift of *xenolalia* (Acts 2.4), and enables inspired and powerful speaking (Acts 4.8,31; 13.9). On the other hand, the Spirit also brings a more general wisdom, a quality that enhances life and enables wise living. Jesus is often said to be 'full of the Holy Spirit' (e.g. Lk. 4.1; 10.21), and both Stephen (see above) and Barnabas (Acts 11.24) are said to be 'full of the Holy Spirit' in the sense that they are people characterised by goodness and faithfulness, rather than any necessarily spectacular ecstatic gifts.

The combination of this Old Testament emphasis on a concentrated level of 'spirit' – life to the *nth* degree, a skill or ability honed over years of training – and the New Testament emphasis on the additional gift of the Spirit over and above any natural human gifting provides an important reminder about the nature of the work of the Spirit in human life. The Spirit inspires both ecstatic experience, sudden abilities to speak in other languages, to effect healings, to have divinely inspired words of knowledge or insight *and* the long-term growth of expertise, ability, intelligence and wisdom concentrated into a significant contribution to the life of a community – in other words, the growth of character. The Spirit is the author of both.

The language of the 'fruit of the Spirit' in Galatians 5 draws particular attention to the extent to which the Spirit forms and shapes character. This is not the realm of the spectacular, the supernatural, the arrival of ecstatic moments of insight or gifts of healing. This instead envisages the growth of characteristics such as 'love, joy, peace, patience, kindness, goodness, faithfulness, gentleness and self-control'. The slow acquisition of these characteristics over time is indicated by the metaphor of fruit, which ripens slowly, not instantly. These are not sudden gifts that appear overnight through a dramatic experience of being 'filled with the Spirit': they are the long-term results of life in the Spirit, formed and cultivated over years of practice: they are the Christian virtues, which are just as markedly the work of the Holy Spirit as the more spectacular phenomena of tongues, signs and wonders.

The New Testament clearly seems to envisage both as works of the Spirit, and leaves them to exist alongside each other, rather than seeing them as in competition or in tension. Now this of course is fully in line with a proper Christian doctrine of creation that sees the Spirit as involved in the ordinary as well as the extraordinary, the natural as well as the supernatural. Both realms are part of creation, and the Spirit is not solely present in one or the other, but rather enhances both realms. There is of course the possibility of Spirit-deficient, stunted and destructive behaviour in the realm of the ecstatic and extraordinary (see for example Simon Magus' attempt to buy the Spirit's power in Acts 8.9–25) just as there is Spirit-deficient, stunted and destructive behaviour in the realm of the rational and ordinary (see the lists of vices scattered throughout the New Testament). The Spirit is not necessarily the author of all things extraordinary and miraculous. He works in and through both the natural and the supernatural, the ordinary and the extraordinary, to bring about the purposes of God.

Seeing the Spirit as the author of the processes that build character and moral excellence over time and also as the one who works through the extraordinary and ecstatic helps us begin to address the question at the heart of this chapter, the question of how we reconcile these two Christian traditions of virtue and goodness. One tradition sees it as the result of an act of faith and the direct work of the Spirit, whilst the other emphasises human co-operation with God. Both, we now see, are works of the Spirit. Yet we still need to explore how these two are related to one another.

The Purpose of Life and Christian Character

The Aristotelian moral tradition defined virtue as that which enables us to achieve our purpose in life, defined as *eudaemonia*, happiness or well-being. The virtuous man is the happy man, the one who exhibits qualities such as courage, temperance, greatness of soul, gentleness, truthfulness, which are all understood as finely balanced on a scale between excess and deficiency (so that generosity for example, is the proper mean between wasteful recklessness and mean stinginess). Character is defined by its goal. In this Greek tradition, prudence, temperance, fortitude and justice are what make for well-being, so that is what we should aim for.

Now Aristotle has a point. Personal transformation has to be organised around a goal, and defining that goal is crucial. There is a great deal of self-help material available in contemporary bookstores, defining human purpose in terms of self-actualisation, personal autonomy or happiness. On the one hand, the goal of life is assumed to be the Disney-inspired path of 'following your dream' or 'being whoever you want to be'. This usually assumes some kind of inner spark, the 'real me' that has been trampled on by the impositions of others, and needs to be released so that I can truly 'find myself'. It is a kind of contemporary gnosticism that posits an unsullied, pure identity at the heart of each human life that has to be discovered and unfettered, so that true happiness can come at last. On the other hand, the goal might be a more corporate version, the utilitarian vision of the libertarian J.S. Mill, the greatest good for the greatest number of people, so that individual strivings for happiness must be modified to fit with the libertarian vision in which my freedom is constrained by the rights of others.

In contrast to these, Christians have a very clear idea of what the goal of human life is, even though it can be described in various ways.[8] One way is to describe it as the restoration of the image of God in humanity. Athanasius's *On the Incarnation* describes the human predicament not so much as needing forgiveness for sins committed but needing a transfusion of divine life, now that sin has initiated a process of corruption into human existence. Humanity once shared the divine image, which was subsequently lost due to disobedience. That image needs to be renewed, which is why God became incarnate in Christ to restore the divine image to a dying and hopeless humanity. Another way to describe essentially the same thing is to say that the goal of human life is to learn to love God and to love our neighbour. It is to take the love that he showers upon us and to reflect it both back to him, and onto our neighbour. More simply perhaps, the goal might simply be described as God himself. Thomas Aquinas argued that the last end of man is *beatitudo*, or happiness, and that happiness is found only in God: 'God is the last end of man and of all other things.'[9]

So far we have explored a further dimension of this sense of purpose. We are here to enable the rest of creation to find healing and fulfil its potential. In order to do that, we need to be united with Christ, which is the work of the Spirit. Yet this is not just in a momentary experience, but if it is to be sustained, needs to work itself out in long-term character. To fulfil our purpose, we need not just to be united to Christ but to grow like him.

Human Destiny and Christian Virtue in Ephesians

The New Testament letter to the Ephesians is one place in the Bible where such themes are taken up and developed. Here, a large-scale, big-canvas picture is painted of God's purpose in all creation, which is to 'bring all things together under one

---

8. See Wright, N. T., *Virtue Reborn* (London: SPCK, 2010) for a useful discussion of virtue in the context of a theology of human purpose.
9. *Summa Theologica*, Ia2æ 1.8.

head, even Christ' (Eph. 1.10). The Greek term used here is the word *anakephalaiōsis* (ανακεφαλαιωσις), usually translated 'recapitulation'. To recapitulate is to repeat, to summarise, or gather up various fragments into a coherent whole. After a long and perhaps rambling speech, a lecturer might say, 'So, to recapitulate ...', meaning she wants to bring order and shape to something which up until that point has lacked it. At the heart of this word is also the Greek word *kefalē* (κεφαλη), or 'head', which is why English translations such as the NIV often use this word in trying to translate an admittedly difficult concept. The idea seems to be that the ultimate purpose of God is to retell the broken story of the whole creation, to give it order, form and coherence by bringing it all under one overarching head: Christ. It is as if all things in their created variety and difference are to be given Christ-like form so that they find the underlying unity that they were created to have, but have lost through the fracturing of creation caused by 'transgressions and sins' (2.1).

In the letter, Paul[10] sees Jesus Christ as the representative human.[11] In his death, the old divided and damaged humanity died with him. Out of the tomb came a new kind of human, or, echoing Milton, Humanity Regained. The Old Testament vision of human calling was to rule over creation, to care for it in God's name (Gn. 1.26; 1.15). Humanity was to act as God's representative, mediating his rule to the rest of creation:

> You made him little lower than the heavenly beings, and crowned him with glory and honour.
> You made him ruler over the works of your hands; you put everything under his feet.

Psalm 8.5–6

This was to be the destiny of humanity. Ephesians 1.20–22 picks up exactly this language, and refers it to the resurrected Christ:

---

10. Without wanting to go into the disputed question of authorship I will assume for the sake of brevity and clarity that Paul is the writer.
11. The 'first Adam' and 'second Adam' language is not used in Ephesians as it is in Romans, however the same train of thought is present.

> ... he raised him from the dead and seated him at his right hand
> in the heavenly realms, far above all rule and authority, power
> and dominion, and every title that can be given, not only in the
> present age, but also in the age to come. And God placed all
> things under his feet and appointed him head over everything for
> the church, which is his body.

In the resurrection of Christ, a new humanity came to birth, humanity as it was always intended to be. However, this is not all. Not only has this renewed humanity finally appeared in the risen Christ, but God has also begun to raise all kinds of individual people *with* Christ, seating them with him in the heavenly realms (2.6). Furthermore he has placed them together in communities that are crucibles of the new humanity. The church, in which the Jewish law, the system of cultural markers that marked off Jew from Gentile, is abolished (2.15), is the place where a new humanity can be reborn with him. The old humanity, divided as it was and is, between Jew and Gentile, slave and free, male and female, is now in principle finished, and the new one has been born: 'His purpose was to create in himself one new humanity out of the two, thus making peace' (2.15). The church is the place where this new humanity is found and nurtured.

As the letter proceeds, Paul outlines his special insight into this mystery, that now is the time for Jews and Gentiles to be brought together into fellowship under Christ in small communities spread around the Mediterranean sea, as a foreshadowing of the day when God will bring all of a divided and broken world together under Christ (3.4–6). Chapters 4–6 are an extended description of what this new humanity actually looks like and how it behaves. It 'makes every effort to keep the unity of the Spirit in the bond of peace' (4.3) because the distinguishing mark of the new humanity is unity and harmony rather than division and disintegration. God gives various gifts with the purpose of enabling the members of the community to 'grow up into him who is the Head, that is, Christ' (4.15).

This new humanity is marked by righteousness and holiness (4.24), truthfulness towards each other (4.25), generosity (4.28), encouragement (4.29), kindness and compassion (4.32). It creates an environment where healthy sexual relationships can flourish (5.2–7), where ecstasy and elation is found not through drink and drugs but through worship and praise (5.18–20). Relationships are marked by mutual submission and honour (5.21) whether in families, or in the workplace (5.22–6.9). And knowing this vision of the new humanity is contested and will be opposed, the community is given the 'full armour of God' to defend itself against all that would aim to thwart God's purposes (6.10–18).

This vision of the development of Christian character, a new way of life, is fully Christological, eschatological and ecclesiological. This new humanity, this new way of living is seen in pristine completeness in the risen Jesus Christ, who is himself the forerunner, the exemplar of humanity reborn as it will one day be. It is ecclesiological in that these communities, gathered around the presence and worship of Christ, are the context in which people are to be raised and reborn through faith (2.8) and reshaped into the Christ-shaped renewed humanity through the exercise of spiritual gifts (4.7–16), paying close attention to Christian teaching (4.14–24) and learning a new spirit and mind (4.23).[12]

The Spirit, Desire, and the New Humanity

The destiny of humanity is to be remade, restored to its original calling to care for creation in God's name, by being united with the risen Christ and growing up into him. In other words, we fulfil our purpose or goal by becoming part of this new humanity, glimpsed in the risen Christ.

What then of the Spirit? As we have already seen, the Holy Spirit's characteristic work is to unite us with Christ, so that we know the love of the Father and become bound up with his

---

12. The Greek here is τω πνευματι του νοος ὑμων (tō pneumatic tou nous ūmōn) – literally, 'in the spirit of your mind'.

mission in the world. We begin to sense the stirring not only
of a response of love to God but also a new sense of calling
towards the world we happen to live in, the communities,
environments and people that we see around us. There are
echoes of exactly this theology in Ephesians. As we saw in
chapter two, Ephesians contains the description of the Spirit
as the 'seal ... a deposit guaranteeing our inheritance until the
redemption of those who are God's possession' (1.14 – see also
4.30). The Holy Spirit is the experience in the present of what
will one day be, and the assurance that God will complete what
he has begun. It is the Spirit who makes knowledge of the risen
Christ possible (1.17).

The Spirit plays a vital role in this Christological vision
of the destiny of humanity. A central section of Ephesians,
marking the transition between the vision of the new humanity
in Christ in the first three chapters and the description of what it
looks like in practice in the last three, is Paul's prayer in 3.14–21.
Significantly, at this pivotal point of the letter, he utters a prayer
for the coming of the Holy Spirit: 'I pray that out of his glorious
riches, he may strengthen you with power through his Spirit
in your inner being ...' The Spirit brings Christ to dwell in the
heart. He makes it possible for us to grasp the love that beats
at the heart of God. He draws us into the love of God, and thus
enables us to be 'filled with all the fullness of God' (3.16–19).
In other words, it is through the Spirit that this transformation
of character happens, by enabling us to experience the depth
and sheer grandeur of the love of God in Christ, the love of
the Father for the Son. The interaction between the experience
of the love of God and the transformation of character stands
right at the heart of this letter and its magnificent vision of
the destiny of creation and the place of humanity in it. What
then is the link between the experience of the Spirit and the
transformation of character?

A key theme here is that of *desire*. In Ephesians, there is an
undercurrent of the significance of desire for the project of the
rebirth of the new humanity. The old humanity is characterised

as 'gratifying the cravings of our sinful nature and following
its desires and thoughts' (2.3). Similarly, the Christian life is
described as learning 'to put off your old self, which is being
corrupted by its deceitful desires' (4.22). The problem is not the
actions, it is the desires that underlie them. Christians are those
in whom new desires have taken root. They are 'renewed in the
Spirit' (4.23), with a new mind, a new self, a new yearning.

A parallel Pauline thought is found in Galatians 5, where
the Holy Spirit is linked to the question of desire: 'So I say,
live by the Spirit, and you will not gratify the desires of the
sinful nature. For the sinful nature desires what is contrary to
the Spirit, and the Spirit what is contrary to the sinful nature.'
(Gal. 5.16–17). The coming of the Spirit brings about a desire
for something new – for 'love, joy, peace, patience, kindness,
goodness, faithfulness, gentleness and self-control' (5.22), rather
than 'hatred, discord, jealousy, fits of rage, selfish ambition,
dissensions, factions and envy; drunkenness, orgies, and the
like' (5.21–22).

The Spirit instils a new desire in the heart, a distaste for
things that once looked so enticing, and a longing for that
which once seemed boring and dull. The true mark of the
presence of the Spirit is the new longings it instils. In answer
to prayer, people can often experience a dramatic sense of the
presence of God, physical healing, or perhaps more disturbing
encounters that unsettle and disorientate. The significance
of those experiences is not so much in themselves (after all,
they are by nature transitory and fleeting), nor just in what
they signify, but in what they leave behind: a new revulsion at
patterns of behaviour that once seemed normal, and a longing
for Christ-likeness, for the good of others and for the kingdom
of Christ.

Now this subtle and small shift in sensibility might seem
insignificant, but it is crucial in the transformation of character.
In a very important sense, we do what we want to do. As St
Augustine above all recognised, desire is fundamental. One of
Augustine's major contentions against the Pelagians was that of

our own free will we cannot desire goodness or God. This alone comes about by the Holy Spirit:

> We however on our side, affirm that the human will is so divinely aided in the pursuit of righteousness that … he receives the Holy Spirit, by whom there is formed in his mind a delight in and love of that supreme and unchangeable good which is God … in order that by this gift to him … he may conceive an ardent desire to cleave to his Creator, and may burn to enter upon the participation in that true light, that it may go well with him from Him to whom he owes his existence.[13]

For Augustine, the work of the Spirit is to reform our desires, to make us long for goodness and hate what is destructive and evil. He insists that only God can do this by the Holy Spirit. Fallen human nature is simply incapable of it – we only desire God when God implants that desire in us. This is the side of the debate that Luther, Calvin and the Reformation theologians emphasised – the priority of grace in the transformation of human life. Yet the result of that transformation of desire is determinedly to pursue goodness in the way that Ephesians recommends. The letter is full of instruction: 'I urge you to live a life …', 'make every effort …', 'you must no longer live as the Gentiles do …', 'you must put off falsehood …', 'Get rid of all bitterness …', 'be very careful how you live …' and so on. This is the side of the debate that is strong in the Aristotelian tradition and among Catholic theologians who stress human co-operation with divine grace. The presupposition of the moral exhortation in Ephesians, however, is the gift of the Spirit who has brought them to life in Christ, who is busy reshaping them into Christ-likeness, and who has already created a new hunger for God and goodness in them.

13. Augustine, *On the Spirit and the Letter* in Warfield, B. B., *Saint Augustine's Anti-Pelagian Works* (Edinburgh: T. & T. Clark), Ch. 5, 84.

The Holy Spirit and the Theology of Virtue

So often in accounts of virtue, the dimension of the Spirit is the missing link. We have already noted the absence of a strong doctrine of the Holy Spirit in Thomas Aquinas. This means his account of the development of virtue is open to Luther's critique that his theology lacked an experiential dimension, that it was too speculative and dry, unable to address the Christian facing sore temptation, doubt or despair. For Luther it was a theology that remained tantalisingly out of reach, unable to address the human heart – it did not make Christ real, did not make him ours. It is ironic then that Luther too has been criticised for having an underdeveloped pneumatology in comparison to christology or his theology of the word. Some recent work has drawn out Luther's doctrine of the Spirit.[14] Burned by his controversies with the enthusiasts, Luther tied the Spirit so closely to the word and the sacrament, that later Lutheranism was sometimes felt to have lost the Spirit in the formalism of preaching and sacramental life to such an extent that the Pietist reaction, restoring an immanent sense of divine encounter, was inevitable.

Even more contemporary theologies that emphasise the importance of virtue as a category for Christian moral reflection and action often display the same omission. Stanley Hauerwas, for example, has a wonderfully creative and bold vision of virtue as opposed to duty or choice as the main way to think about Christian action in the world. It is exhilarating and makes a huge deal of sense. However, there is a distinct lack of a developed theology of the Holy Spirit in his approach that leaves the feeling that you are never quite sure how virtue actually grows.[15] Hauerwas argues that for Christian character to develop it is vital to live in a community in which a distinct narrative is present: 'it demands that we acquire a narrative that

---

14. In particular, Prenter, R., *Spiritus Creator: Luther's Concept of the Holy Spirit*.
15. This lack of pneumatology in Hauerwas' work has been noticed by, among others, Bretherton, L., *Hospitality as Holiness: Christian Witness amid Moral Diversity* (Aldershot: Ashgate, 2006), 106; and Hütter, R., 'Ecclesial Ethics, the Church's Vocations, and Paraclesis' *Pro Ecclesia* 2 (1993), 450.

gives us the skill to fit what we do and do not do into a coherent
account sufficient to claim our life as our own … internal to the
story itself is the claim that we cannot know the story simply
by hearing it, but only by learning to imitate those who now
are the continuation of the story.'[16] To be sure, imitating other
Christians is a vital means of developing virtue, but what
makes me *want* to imitate them, as opposed to any other group
of people I may be close to? The missing dimension here is how
we begin to indwell the story, how it becomes not just another
story out there, but my story, one in which I live and which
makes sense of my life. The answer to these questions has to
be the work of the Holy Spirit, who touches hearts, minds and
bodies, making us one with Christ, conveying a sense of the
felt presence and power of God, and giving birth to a desire to
seek Christ-like life, to imitate the life patterns of the Christian
community, and to long for Christian virtue.

The Prodigal Spirit, Experience and Character

The prodigal Spirit reaches out from the heart of God to
draw us into the love between the Father and the Son. A true
encounter with that Spirit kindles a desire for God and the
things of God. It draws us into Christ not only so that we know
the love of the Father, not only so that we find a new purpose
in life, joining in his mission in the world, but so that we might
pursue Christ-likeness of character, formed into the life of
Christ, the new humanity. The result, in very ordinary day-to-
day terms, is new disciplines of prayer, the reading of Scripture,
engaging in Christian community, silence, celebration,
confession, worship. These classic Christian disciplines are
the means through which character is developed. Aquinas,
Hauerwas and other theologians who emphasise virtue see this
clearly, yet it is vital not to miss the crucial role of the Spirit in
stimulating the desire to pursue Christ and his life.

If we are to be capable of fulfilling the calling of humanity

---

16. Hauerwas, S., *A Community of Character: Toward a Constructive Christian Social Ethic* (Notre
Dame: University of Notre Dame, 1981), 151f.

to work with God towards the healing and fulfilment of creation, that will require a level of transformation of inner life, motivation and character that goes beyond a momentary experience to a lifelong, settled pattern of life. In other words, if we are to be united with Christ so that we share in his calling towards the world, that will mean a gradual conformity to Christ so that this stance towards the world becomes a habitual, daily inclination. The knowledge of the Father's love will need to become so embedded and sure in us that it is rarely doubted and becomes the stable bedrock of daily life, moment-by-moment, consciously or unconsciously. Reacting to congenial or difficult people, simple or complicated situations, with that same love and compassion will need to become a normal, regular tendency.

The experience of the Spirit is a crucial and indispensable element in the development of character capable of bearing witness to Christ. Yet the experience is just the start. It is like the spark that ignites the engine, the glimpse that inspires the search. The two are connected in that the experience of the Spirit is not an end in itself, but becomes the beginning of a process of transformation of character. If the Spirit's work is to make us one with Christ, then that will mean a new knowledge of the love of God and a new calling of service and suffering for the world he loves. The long-term result of this union with Christ by the Spirit will also be the establishing of these same transformed relationships with both God and the world into steady, settled, regular patterns of life, through patterns of Christian discipline, attention to Christian teaching and the exercise of spiritual gifts. Virtue or character, the steady, settled habits of life that exhibit frequent acts of kindness, humility, forgiveness and love begin to emerge when the Spirit draws us into the love between the Father and the Son, which is his characteristic work. It will become second nature to know and assume the love of the Father, second nature to act toward the world or your awkward neighbour with compassion and grace. Like brushing your teeth in the morning, it is not something you keep forgetting, but instead becomes part of you.

Now there is of course a danger here, that of presuming on the love and grace of God. However, there is a difference between presumption and assurance. Presumption is where God's grace becomes ordinary, expected, even deserved. It is the attitude of Heinrich Heine's famous statement: 'Of course God will forgive: that's his job.' Presumption is when we begin to forget the unexpected, miraculous, undeserved, wonderful nature of grace. Assurance is when we retain that sense of wonder as a natural way of life, and we learn to live out of it daily.

Does this happen instantly or gradually? Well, the answer is probably both. Many people, on encountering a powerful sense of the love of God for the first time, feel that everything has changed. The language of being 'born again' captures the sense that everything seems new, they find a new love for God and for people welling up inside them, the world suddenly seems charged with the presence of God, and they feel a new person instantly. However, it is usually the case that such a feeling does not last. As in the parable of the Sower, the cares of life, the lures of trivial attractions such as money, sex, fame and power make such an experience fade and dissipate. A natural reaction can be to try constantly to repeat the initial experience of overwhelming change, constantly to search for the original spiritual 'high', yet while a repeated expression of dependence on the Spirit is vital, what is really required is for the state of mind and heart first experienced in the moment of encounter to become a settled pattern of life.

If the work of the Spirit is to unite us with Christ, to make us one with him, so that we enter into the same relationship that he has with both the Father and the world, then an inevitable outcome of this is not only that we will experience this, but that we will find ourselves becoming conformed to Christ as a long-term settled pattern of life, not just as a momentary experience. What we know instinctively in moments of worshipful praise, the experience of the presence and power of God, the numinous sense of the Spirit's working upon us, becomes not just an occasional spiritual 'trip', but a steady way of life, fuelled by a new desire to be like Christ. We do not live in a constant stream of ecstatic experience, but we are to live in the Spirit, the Spirit who unites us with Christ and makes us one with him in experience and in character.

CHAPTER 5

THE HOLY SPIRIT AND EVANGELISM

We have been exploring how the Spirit works in human life and how that life is transformed by the presence and power of the Spirit. The discussion so far has focused on the work of the Spirit within Christian people and within the church. How then might this be translated into a set of practices that help the church engage with the world? In the first instance, this raises the question of evangelism, and how this ministry might be understood, seen from a pneumatological perspective.

Churches need to take evangelism seriously, if only for the sake of their own integrity. It is one thing for a group of people to hold a belief in God the Father, Son and Holy Spirit. Yet how do you know whether they really mean it? How can you tell whether such a belief is merely a subjective private choice, rather than a belief in the *truth* of what they say they believe? What is the sign that they really believe this to be true in the fullest sense, not just a private truth for themselves but true for the whole world? The answer is to look at their willingness to let such a belief be known. Lesslie Newbigin wrote: 'The test of our real belief is our readiness to share it with all peoples.'[1] It is a sign of health in a church to hold a strong desire to reach out beyond itself to extend the invitation to know the transforming love of God to those who do not yet know it. It is

---

1. Newbigin, L., *The Gospel in a Pluralist Society* (London: SPCK, 1989), 126.

a sure indication of proper intellectual and spiritual integrity. Newbigin's point is that when you find a church that engages in evangelism in some significant but sensitive way, seeking to share Christ with others, that is an indication that that church really believes what it says it does, and believes that he is the way, the truth and the life. It thinks that what it believes is the truth for the whole world, not just for itself.

So evangelism is a crucial ministry for the health and integrity of the church. The word 'evangelism' is one of those words that conjures up in most Europeans and Americans negative images of very uncool zealotry. What might evangelism look like in the light of this Trinitarian and eschatological theology of the Spirit? Might this approach help develop a more rounded and culturally sensitive form of evangelism? This chapter explores these issues using one particular phenomenon – the Alpha course – as a case study of a style of evangelism that has been very significant for many churches in recent years. Alpha has been the route through which countless people across the world have found faith since it began to spread beyond its base in Holy Trinity Brompton in London in the early 1990s. This Trinitarian pneumatology might help us understand why it has been so significant, and examine some of its implicit theological rationale.

Evangelism as Encounter

If the Spirit's work is to draw the whole of creation into the transforming love of God, the love between the Father and the Son; if identity and vocation are discovered through being united with Christ through the Holy Spirit, then the heart of evangelism will be more than the impartation of theological information, or the urging to moral renewal: it will be the facilitation of an encounter with God.[2]

---

2. Cartledge, M. J., *Encountering the Spirit: The Charismatic Tradition* (London: Darton, Longman & Todd) helpfully identifies this sense of encounter with God as one of the key features of charismatic Christianity, and hence one of its main gifts to the wider church.

The Holy Spirit is, as it were, our gateway into God. The Spirit is the one who invites us into relationship with God, into the love between the Father and the Son. This, as we have seen in the previous chapters, is something to be experienced, so that evangelism needs to enable an encounter that goes beyond mere knowledge. It is an encounter that may be mediated by some of the classic Christian means of grace, such as teaching, prayer, the laying on of hands, even sacramental ministry, but all the time maintaining a sense that the Spirit blows where he wills, and leaving a strong degree of freedom for the Spirit to act independently of human control.

Evangelism has often focused on an invitation to 'invite Jesus into my heart'. More recent forms of evangelism, such as that found in the Alpha course, shift the focus to the prayer 'Come Holy Spirit'. This indicates a theological shift, from human decision as the main driver in coming to faith (my decision to 'invite Jesus in' being central), to God as the main actor in the process. Asking the Spirit to enable the seeker to know the love of the Father in Christ (Jn. 16.14–15) is an important theocentric shift of focus, recognising that faith is a gift of the Spirit, and that unless the Spirit is at work, faith cannot be born.

Yet there is a tension in this theme of evangelism as encounter with God, which centres around the theme of the freedom of the Spirit. One of the seminal texts in the gospels on the Holy Spirit comes in the conversation between Jesus and Nicodemus in John 3, where Jesus says:

> No one can enter the kingdom of God unless he is born of water and the Spirit. Flesh gives birth to flesh, but the Spirit gives birth to spirit. You should not be surprised at my saying, 'You must be born again.' The wind blows wherever it pleases. You hear its sound, but you cannot tell where it comes from or where it is going. So it is with everyone born of the Spirit.

John 3.5–8

Because he is the Spirit who brings the future into the present, he brings something entirely new into the arena of human life. Precisely because it is new, it is something we cannot entirely envisage or control. The Spirit jealousy guards his freedom from human control.

And yet, the Spirit is given freely. Jesus in Luke's Gospel says: 'If you then, though you are evil, know how to give good gifts to your children, how much more will your Father in heaven give the Holy Spirit to those who ask him!' (Lk. 11.13). In John, the same pledge is expressed: 'God gives the Spirit without limit' (Jn. 3.34). The Spirit is Gift, given without reluctance. God promises to give or send his Spirit when asked. We cannot control the Spirit, but he is still promised when we ask. The Spirit is free, both in the sense that he remains free from human control, and yet he is given freely when requested: the Spirit is free, but not random.

This tension is brought out by a story recounted in Acts chapter 8. Some Samarian converts had been baptised into the name of Jesus, but the Spirit had not yet come upon them. So, Peter and John are sent to Samaria, where the Spirit comes on these new disciples when the apostles lay hands on them. Watching this, Simon the magician, on his conversion, asks if he can buy the Holy Spirit's power from the apostles. He is rebuked in no uncertain terms, because he has sought to own the Spirit, to bring the Spirit under his control with his money. The tension lies in the fact that the apostles are, it seems, able to convey the Spirit through the laying on of their hands and through prayer, and yet at the same time the Spirit cannot be possessed, owned or bought with money. The same tension is found elsewhere in the Scriptures: God's power works through the performance of the sacraments, through preaching, through the laying on of hands and through prayer (Luke 4.40; Acts 8.18; 9.17f; 2 Tim. 1.6 etc.). All of these are on one level at least, human actions subject to human decision. We decide when and whether to baptise, preach, pray, lay on hands and so on. Yet at the same time, as John 3.8 reminds us, God retains a sovereign liberty to act independently and *despite*, rather than only *through*, human means. Human actions do not guarantee the working of the Spirit. The Spirit responds to human action, yet retains a freedom from human control. The Spirit works through us but is not controlled by us.

This tension lies at the heart of many a dispute in the history of the church. On the one hand, many Christians have emphasised the authorised channels through which the Spirit moves, the means of grace, the sacraments, authorised liturgy, prayer and gestures. Others have emphasised the utter freedom of the Spirit from human control. A classic example is the dispute between Luther and Zwingli over the sacraments in the sixteenth century. Luther insisted, on the grounds of the incarnation, that the Spirit works through physical things. God's primary mode of self-revelation in the world was the flesh of Jesus Christ. So, we should expect this to continue to be the way in which God makes himself known to us – in the physical form of the bread and wine of the Eucharist, in which Christ is really and physically present. Luther says of his opponents: 'They think nothing spiritual can be present where there is anything material and physical, and assert that flesh is of no avail. Actually the opposite is true. The Spirit cannot be with us except in material and physical things such as the Word, water, and Christ's body and in his saints on earth.'[3] Zwingli on the other hand wanted to assert the absolute freedom of the Spirit from human control, fearing that Luther and his followers wanted to restrict the Spirit to human action. Zwingli asserted repeatedly the importance of both John 3.8, ('the Spirit blows where he pleases'), and also John 6.63: 'The Spirit gives life; the flesh counts for nothing.'

In fact, on closer analysis, the dispute perhaps need not have split the Reformation movement as it did. Luther's own theology of the Holy Spirit shows a subtle distinction between the human delivery of the word and the action of the Spirit through it. Luther did indeed teach that the Spirit comes through outward signs, yet he also knew that the Spirit was

3. Pelikan, J.; Oswald, H. C.; Lehmann, H. T., *Luther's Works, Vol. 37: Word and Sacrament III* (Philadelphia : Fortress Press, 1999), 95.

not tied to such signs. The word alone for Luther is merely the law. It is when the Spirit comes upon it to make it live, that it becomes gospel. Regin Prenter speaks of a vital 'hiatus', a kind of theological interval between the preaching of the word and the coming of the Spirit. The same is true, he argues, for the sacraments: the Spirit uses sacramental signs, yet remains sovereign over them. If we claim that the Spirit comes by virtue of our own action when we preach or celebrate the sacraments, this places too much emphasis on the preacher or the priest, ensnaring Christian ministry within the sense of automatic sacramental operation that Luther had rejected in the medieval church's understanding of sacramental action *ex opere operato*. God has indeed bound himself to these actions and external signs, yet we must always hold to the 'sovereignty of the Spirit over the external signs' and the ultimate 'insufficiency of the outward Word.' The Spirit does not come without the Word, but he is not bound by the Word.[4]

The Spirit works through human agency, yet is not confined or controlled by human action. Properly speaking, the Spirit is at work throughout Christian worship, through praise, the sermon, the sacraments, the fellowship and all the other activities that take place when Christians gather together. All this expresses one aspect of the tension: that the Spirit works through human activity, through the means of grace. Yet there comes a point when it is appropriate to stop, to lay down human activity, to keep silence and to wait for the Spirit, to give the Spirit space to work in freedom. Traditional liturgical structures that allow no opportunity for the Spirit to do or say anything other than what has been previously scripted are perhaps guilty of failing to observe and to maintain the biblical tension in the theology of the Spirit between human agency and divine freedom.[5] Similarly, worship that has no structure at all lacks a sense of the presence of Christ through the Spirit in word and sacrament and fails to hold the other side of this

---

4. Prenter, R., *Spiritus Creator: Luther's Concept of the Holy Spirit.*
5. Jürgen Moltmann suggests that classic Reformation theologies of justification need to be re-worked and re-presented, so that they have greater focus on Resurrection and eschatology *and* 'must be presented pneumatologically as experience of the Spirit.' Moltmann, J., *The Spirit of Life: A Universal Affirmation* (London: SCM, 1992), 149.

tension. The invitation to the Spirit to come during the offering of worship, in the context of the preaching of the word or the administration of the sacraments, is one way of maintaining a vital place for human agency, yet allowing space for the freedom of the Spirit.

The church cannot presume on the Spirit. At times it has taken for granted that by doing certain liturgical acts, performing certain gestures or uttering wise words, that the Spirit will automatically come, *ex opere operato*, as it were. And yet it can rely on the promise that God will send his Spirit. How is this tension to be properly maintained in the church's life? The answer surely is: by invocation. Neither individual Christians nor the church as a whole possess the Spirit. Asking is part of the way in which the Spirit is given. We always need to ask, and to ask continually. The necessity of asking expresses this vital dimension of the freedom of the Spirit from human control, yet his willingness at the same time to be tied to and work through human agency.

The church has always prayed this prayer. The *Veni Creator Spiritus*, one of the classic Christian prayers, invites the Spirit to fill human hearts:

> Come, Holy Spirit, Creator blest
> And in our souls take up Thy rest
> Come with Thy grace and heavenly aid
> To fill the hearts which Thou hast made.

The song then asks the Spirit to anoint us with his sevenfold gifts of understanding, knowledge, wisdom, counsel, piety, fortitude, and the fear of the Lord:[6]

> Come, Holy Ghost, our souls inspire
> And lighten with celestial fire
> Thou the anointing Spirit art
> Who dost Thy sevenfold gifts impart.

---

6. This traditional list comes from Is. 11.1–2.

This practice of invocation of the Spirit has helped the church avoid two equally dangerous forms of presumption: blithely taking for granted the presence of the Spirit, or acting as if the Spirit was not necessary and that we can do it all ourselves. Moltmann puts it well: 'The relation of the church to the Holy Spirit is the relation of *epiklesis*, continual invocation of the Spirit and unconditional opening for the experiences of the Spirit who confers fellowship and who makes life truly worth living.'[7]

The invocation of the Spirit is a key element of charismatic and eucharistic worship. However, space needs to be found not only in liturgical or worshipful settings, but also evangelistic ones, for this invocation of the Spirit. If Christian faith begins with an encounter with God through the Spirit, bring brought by the Spirit into the love between the Father and the Son, then this needs to be part of any evangelistic process, as for example, happens on the Alpha course on the weekend away. It is vital at the moment of invocation not to manipulate or control what happens, despite the temptation to do so. The silence that falls at that point is a crucial one. To claim that when the Spirit is invited, he comes, is an expression of confidence in the Spirit's responsiveness to the church's prayers, not an attempt to control the Spirit, nor a prediction of how exactly the Spirit will make his presence felt. Invocation of the Spirit needs to be an essential part of the evangelistic process, asking the Spirit to bring to life what has been taught, shared, known, inviting the Spirit to bring a new intimate knowledge of the love of God in Christ and a new purpose to be and act like him.

Evangelism as Catechesis

Many, if not most recent approaches to evangelism have moved from the general idea of conversion as a crisis to conversion

7. Moltmann, *The Spirit of Life*, 230.

as a process.[8] This is often linked to changes in culture. The suggestion is that now people in Western societies generally know less about the basics of Christian faith, it takes longer for them to know what they are being invited into, so courses that take time to build up understanding are more likely to be effective than one-off events such as the great evangelistic crusades of the 1950s and 60s, which aimed to produce instant conversions on the night. This may well explain what is happening on 'process courses' in evangelism, but there are other more theological and philosophical approaches to this trend that are worth exploring as well, in particular the suggestion that the invitation to faith is an invitation not to adopting a set of ideas, liturgical practices or moral commitments, but to life in the Spirit.

There is an evidentialist approach to evangelism that suggests that it is possible to demonstrate the truth of Christian faith through the use of careful argument or apologetics. This approach relies on there being agreed and demonstrable foundations for knowledge that exist independently of Christian faith. The evangelist or apologist has to appeal to these universal foundations to show that Christianity passes the test of truth, and can verify its claims accordingly.

Increasing numbers of Christian thinkers and writers have raised doubts about this approach in recent years. Theologians such as Hans Frei, George Lindbeck, Stanley Hauerwas, Nicholas Wolterstorff and Alvin Plantinga all in different ways agree that the search for universal foundations for knowledge and truth outside of Christian belief is questionable. As we have seen already by looking briefly at Plantinga's thought, for him, faith does not rest on argumentation or logical inference from first principles, but is 'properly basic', needing no external grounding, and comes by the gift of the Holy Spirit. Ludwig Wittgenstein famously argued that the best analogy for religion

---

8. Finney, J., *Finding Faith Today: How Does it Happen?* (Swindon: BFBS, 1992) contained a small but vital piece of research that focused attention on this new approach to evangelism. Abraham, W. J., *The Logic of Evangelism* (London: Hodder, 1989), was a seminal book that shifted thinking on evangelism towards the idea that evangelism itself is a process of initiation rather than a one-off crisis event.

is that it is like a language. A language cannot be understood from outside, but it has to be learnt by speaking it and listening to it. It has to be lived in, conversed in. We do not learn Chinese by looking at English translations of Chinese texts – we have to start speaking and reading and listening to Chinese. For Wittgenstein, Christian doctrines are like the rules of grammar that govern a language, the explanation of how it works.

To illustrate this, we might ask a question: in a pluralist society, how are we meant to decide between different religious claims? How might someone decide to be a Christian as opposed to a Buddhist, a Muslim or an atheist? Can we take each of these systems of thought to the bar of reason, evaluating them all against a set of agreed criteria, rational or experiential, for accepting their relative claims to truth, as the philosophers of the Enlightenment claimed to be able to do? This is of course to assume that there is a separate standard of rationality beyond Christian doctrine to which it must bow and before which it must put its claims, a rationality or logic that thus becomes higher and more authoritative than Christian revelation itself. Even if it were argued that God has implanted foundational reason in us so that the claims of Christian faith can still be proved to be true, many theologians, particularly of a more Augustinian bent, would argue that our ability to perceive them is so damaged by sin's effects on our minds, that we cannot usefully appeal to them. If the attempt to find indubitable foundations for knowledge, a way of proving Christian faith to be true once and for all, is ultimately fruitless, then another way needs to be found.

To take Wittgenstein's analogy further, the only way we can decide on the truth of a particular view of the world is by trying it on, indwelling it, learning to live inside it – a bit like learning Chinese by going to China and starting to speak it for ourselves. Naturally, anyone approaching Christian faith, or any other way of life and thought for that matter, wants to examine it, look around it from the outside, see whether it stacks up or makes some kind of sense. However, this approach can only take you so far. The only way to learn a faith is to follow up a hunch that it might just be true, by beginning to live it, to indwell it.

Imagine a traveller approaching a sea with various islands dotted around it. How might she work out which is the best island to live on? One possibility might to be take a plane, fly above the islands and make a judgement from above, assessing the relative merits of each. The 'view from above' is theoretically possible, but it does rather rely on having a plane. If such a plane were unavailable, she would have to try another way. She might sail around, looking at each one in turn, but at the end of the day, she has to find somewhere to live, and the only real way of finding out is actually setting up home on one of the islands that looks as if it might be a good one. Only when she lands, tries it out, sees what the view is like, how fertile the soil is, what materials there are for building, can she really tell whether she has made a good choice. Of course she may have made a bad choice, finding that life is really unsustainable on this island, and she needs to move to another. But the point is that she can only find this out by actually trying to live there.

Likewise with the choice about faith. If there is no universal standpoint from which the relative merits of various religious or philosophical choices might be assessed, the only way forward is to make a choice as to which way looks promising and then start living within a particular path of life and faith, adopting its practices and trying it out. If so, while evangelism will need to include some basic apologetics to those still looking in from outside (just checking from a distance whether the island looks worth a try), its main focus will be catechesis to those who have already joined. In other words, the church extends the invitation to join the Christian community in a tentative and provisional way, start to live its way of life and speak its language, before a real decision can be made as to whether to set up home here, to become a Christian.

This is of course, how the early church did its evangelism – by catechesis. If you were interested in Christian faith, like the young Augustine arriving in Milan to start his new career in rhetoric, you didn't just read books about it, but you joined the catechumenate. This was the early church's means of ensuring new Christians knew what they were letting themselves in for. Those interested in Christianity would join the ranks of the catechumens, those being taught the way of Christ in preparation for baptism, the point at which they would enter the Christian church properly.

The catechetical process varied a great deal from place to place, and across the different eras of the patristic period, including questions of the stage at which baptism was introduced in the process, sometimes fairly early on, at other times after a three-year process of initiation, at others delayed until just before death. Generally, however, the content of catechesis was a mixture of moral, spiritual and doctrinal teaching. Catechumens could be gathered together for instruction as part of the community celebrations early in the morning. The basic requirements of Christian life were laid out, spiritual disciplines recommended and the basics of Christian belief explained. Generally speaking, the process continued through various stages leading up to baptism and admittance to the Eucharist, with personal examinations at the end of each.[9] Interestingly, un-baptised catechumens were normally regarded as Christians, even though they were not yet admitted to full participation in the Eucharist.[10]

The catechumenate blends together evangelism with spiritual formation. These go together once Christian faith is understood as a way of life to be learnt, rather than a set of ideas to be agreed with. George Lindbeck comments how in the early church, instruction on the Christian faith began after people had tentatively joined the Christian community, not before:

> Pagan converts to the catholic mainstream did not, for the most part, first understand the faith and then decide to become

---

9. See Dujarier, M., *A History of the Catechumenate: The First Six Centuries* (New York, Sadlier, 1979).
10. See Hall, S. G., *Doctrine and Practice in the Early Church* (London: SPCK, 1991), 15.

Christians; rather the process was reversed: they first decided and then they understood. More precisely, they were first attracted by the Christian Community and form of life ... they submitted themselves to prolonged catechetical instruction in which they practised new modes of behaviour and learned the stories of Israel and their fulfilment in Christ. Only after they had acquired proficiency in the alien Christian language and form of life were they deemed able intelligently and responsibly to profess the faith, to be baptised.[11]

Tory Baucum helpfully explores the importance of catechesis in evangelism.[12] He explores early Methodism and the Alpha course, describing the latter as a rediscovery of the catechetical approach to evangelism for a new missionary context.[13] He highlights the missing link in much contemporary evangelism, the ability of churches to provide 'cultures of faith' or a 'participatory, interpersonally rich context where people learn to connect authentically with God and one another.'[14] His point is that unless churches can create such spaces where faith can be learnt and explored, evangelism will usually fail, because of the nature of the message being communicated. Because the gospel is an invitation to know a personal and relational God, it can only be communicated in personal and relational ways, ways that have the crucial quality of hospitable friendship at their heart, a factor that is observably true both of the early Wesleyan movement and also of Alpha.

Without demanding too neat a fit between contemporary forms of evangelism and specific forms of early church catechesis, this is what an evangelistic process needs to provide today. It needs to offer a place of belonging, a 'plausibility shelter' to use Duncan MacLaren's phrase,[15] in which those who want to explore Christian faith can not only find sustained

---

11. Lindbeck, G., *The Nature of Doctrine* (New Haven: Yale University Press), 132.
12. Baucum, T., *Evangelical Hospitality: Catechetical Evangelism in the Early Church and its Recovery for Today* (Lanham, ML: Scarecrow Press, 2008).
13. *Ibid.*, 185.
14. *Ibid.*, 13.
15. MacLaren, D., *Mission Implausible: Restoring Credibility to the Church* (Milton Keynes: Paternoster, 2004).

exposure to its ideas and doctrines, but can begin to try them on, and begin to live them.

Again, perhaps one of the reasons why Alpha has been so successful is that is provides such a 'plausibility shelter'. On the very first week of an Alpha course, sceptical attendees are invited to join in Christian worship (few do, of course, but the invitation is there). After only three or four weeks, people start learning about prayer, Scripture reading, discernment of the will of God and so on. By that stage, few sceptics or unbelievers are necessarily convinced enough to be ready to fully sign up to Christian faith. Is it appropriate to ask someone to engage in these Christian practices before they have been fully convinced or fully initiated by baptism into the Christian church?

The approach we have been exploring above suggests that this makes perfect sense. Christian faith is learnt not just as a set of ideas examined from outside, but as a way of life to be explored from within. It is life in the Spirit, life lived with a new identity and new vocation. It is like buying a coat. Few people will take one look at an expensive coat in shop, hand over the money and walk out. Most will want to try it on for size and comfort, see how it feels and looks, before making the purchase. Becoming a Christian, adopting this new identity and vocation is in many ways just like this. That is why adopting a stricter approach to initiation, such as insisting on baptism, or some kind of public statement of faith as a precondition for involvement in church life and beginning Christian practice seldom works. It assumes a foundational approach to knowledge, fails to take into account the nature of Christian faith as a way of life learnt and inhabited, and ignores the wide variety of routes people take into Christian faith, especially in a post-Christian culture like ours.

If coming to faith were simply a matter of deciding which island I like best, which has the better view, then that decision might still be made on quite selfish or limited grounds. The self might then remain untouched, adopting the best lifestyle that fits an essentially self-centred view of the world. On the contrary, the proclamation of the gospel is an invitation to a new identity and a new calling. It invites us to start to live this new life. The evangelistic process thus provides not only the context for such gradual acclimatisation to Christian faith, but also the possibility of moral and spiritual renewal so that the entry into Christian faith can involve a transformation of the heart, not just a personal lifestyle choice like buying a better car, home or mobile phone.

Evangelism today needs to offer the opportunity to try faith out for a while, and at the same time open oneself to the action of the Spirit. To use the Alpha course as an example again, on the first evening a guest is put into a group hosted by a couple of Christians, giving her a first experience of Christian relationships. She begins to learn how worship works. During the session on prayer she is invited to begin to pray and be prayed for. She begins to hear Christian teaching, and maybe even starts to read the Bible for herself at home. She encounters Christian prayer for healing, and how to recognise and resist the destructive power of evil. She tentatively opens her heart to the Holy Spirit's gentle influence, and begins to experience the love of God and the pain of the world. In other words, this is a bite-sized and authentic experience of Christian life and community, identity and vocation. It is missing the point to insist that a person should wait until they are convinced or understand enough, or make some kind of formal commitment to Christ before they can pray or worship, because Christian faith is a way of life. Instead, this approach offers the opportunity for an iterative process of discovery, which leads towards formal initiation through baptism or another rite of entry, rather than presuming it from the beginning.

Evangelism as Hospitality

At the heart of this book is a relational Trinitarianism that sees the love between the Father and the Son at the very centre of reality, with the Holy Spirit as extending an invitation to the rest of creation to be part of that loving embrace. This is a view of the world that places welcome, invitation and hospitality at the centre of everything.

The theme of hospitality has been a fruitful area of theological exploration in recent years. For Luke Bretherton, hospitality is a more fruitful mode for Christians to engage with others in moral dialogue than mere 'tolerance', as it shows how ethical questions can be seen in a completely new light in the welcoming presence of God.[16] Amos Yong considers hospitality as a way of engaging in inter-faith encounter, where Christians are sometimes guests, sometimes hosts, in such a way that gives space for the Spirit to work in both contexts.[17] Christine Pohl explores hospitality as a properly subversive and deeply Christian practice.[18] As seen already, Tory Baucum explores the theme of hospitality as the main dynamic at work in the Alpha course. All four authors see hospitality as a culturally and theologically appropriate means of Christian engagement with those outside the church.

Evangelism needs to be done communally and hospitably. Yet often in the past, that has not always been the case. Evangelism has sometimes taken the form of inviting people to listen to a lecture, giving little space for the kind of thing that commonly happens at parties, shared meals or home visits – conversation, questions and the sharing of stories. If evangelism is in theological terms an invitation into the realm of the love of God, then it will naturally create space for hospitable conversation.

One of the characteristic pieces of advice given during training for leaders of the groups for discussion on Alpha is that they should not be too quick to give the answer to anyone raising questions about or objections to faith. Instead they need to ensure that there is a proper process of listening. The guests

16. Bretherton, L., *Hospitality as Holiness: Christian Witness Amid Moral Diversity*. (Aldershot: Ashgate, 2006).

17. Yong, A., *Hospitality and the Other: Pentecost, Christian Practices, and the Neighbor* (New York: Orbis, 2008).

18. Pohl, C., *Making Room: Recovering Hospitality as a Christian Tradition* (Grand Rapids: Eerdmans, 1999).

have already heard a talk on Christian faith – they do not need
to hear another, but instead need now to be heard, rather than
spoken to again. This approach has been criticised for the way
it can leave guests a little frustrated at not getting responses to
their legitimate questions, and there may be some merit in the
charge.[19] However, the rationale for the advice to encourage
conversation rather than give direct answers is that too hasty
an answer shuts down discussion and inhibits exploration.
It is all too easy to rush in to give facile and shallow answers
to deeply felt questions. It is also vital to allow guests the
freedom to speak, to say what is on their hearts, to express their
frustrations with God and the church. The task of the leader is
first and foremost to listen. The granting of this freedom is so
vital that it is worth risking a guest feeling their questions are
not receiving answers. If one has to err on one side, it is better
to allow that freedom than to close down expression and start
preaching at people again.

This openness to questions can be seen as a reflection of the
incarnation and the sending of the Spirit. In the Word become
flesh in Jesus Christ, God opens himself to human questioning.
Jesus does not just preach at people, he allows them to
question him and engage in conversation, with the flow of the
conversation often taking the form of further questions. In the
person of Christ, you could actually address your questions
to God directly! This welcoming of questions is unusual in
Christian evangelism where often the stress is on the other
side – getting over the information so that the other person is
in no doubt of what they are meant to believe. This readiness to
make space for questions, and even to leave them unresolved
at times, comes from a conviction that at the end of the day
what an unbeliever really needs is not a satisfying answer to
their questions, but an encounter with God. Of course, finding
sensible and thoughtful answers to those questions can help
clear the way for such an encounter, but fundamentally, these
answers are a means to an end, not an end in themselves.

Most people have stories of fleeting encounters with God

---

19. Heard, J., 'Re-evangelising Britain? An Ethnographic Analysis and Theological Evaluation of
the Alpha Course' (PhD diss., King's College London, 2007), 159f.

in the past, events that have pointed them towards faith or away from it, objections that prevent them from believing. The would-be evangelist has to learn the discipline of listening closely to such stories, just like a good host encouraging a guest to speak their mind, refraining from turning the conversation to topics the host is interested in, running the discussion entirely on their own terms.[20]

The best evangelism finds ways of convening and enabling a conversation in which truth can be discovered. It encourages the hospitality of listening. Good conversations are always two-sided. Of course this balance is often hard to maintain. Some evangelistic encounters, whether in an Alpha group or elsewhere, lean too far in the direction of silencing discussion, closing down questions like a rude host never quite allowing anyone to have opinions other than their own. Others lean too far in the direction of never offering anything to continue the conversation, failing to offer cogent and thoughtful replies to valid questions, enabling a good healthy process of discovery. Alpha at its best is an example of evangelism that seeks to extend hospitality to guests, to mirror God's welcome to a broken world. Hospitality by its very nature does not force itself upon people. In some ways it is a healthy sign if some people coming on Alpha courses do not end up as Christians or part of a church. If a guest chooses to leave after a week or two, no one rings to hassle them into coming back, or make them feel guilty for lack of commitment. That is what hospitality does – it provides a context for conversation, for encounter and thus for transformation in that encounter with God, his church and the gospel.

The gospel is an act of hospitality in which we discover who we are. Christ follows us into the far country to make a way back to God. The prodigal Spirit follows along the same trails to woo us back into the embrace of God. Being welcomed into the life of God, into the love between the Father and the Son

20. Alpha is sometimes critiqued for being too prescriptive and pre-packaged. See Percy, M. '"Join-the-dots" Christianity: Assessing ALPHA.' *Reviews in Religion and Theology* 4 (1997): 14–18; Hunt, S., *Anyone for Alpha?* (London: Darton, Longman & Todd, 2001). Yet this critique tends to miss the genuine openness that exists in Alpha groups when they work at their best, and the sense of balance that exists on a good Alpha evening between proclamation and open-ended questioning.

through the Spirit, we discover we are loved in a way we never imagined – we are the treasured sons and daughters of God. We also discover what we are meant to be doing – extending that hospitality to a world that has wandered far from its true home. If hospitality is that central to the gospel, it has to be central to evangelism.

Evangelism as Anticipation

Our earlier reflections on the theology of the Holy Spirit emphasised its eschatological dimension, especially in the teaching of St Paul. The Spirit is a first instalment of the future, a downpayment of the inheritance to come. At the same time, Jesus' announcement of the kingdom of God, come in his own person and ministry, was itself a foretaste of the future day of resurrection when the kingdom will come in its fullness. Christian life therefore always has this note of expectant waiting, where the experience of the future is accessible yet always a little tantalising, frustrating and incomplete. In Christian faith and experience we are given something, but not everything.

This is expressed sacramentally in the Holy Communion, Lord's Supper or Eucharist. This is a meal that anticipates the end. St Paul's account of the meal claims that every time Christians meet around bread and wine, they 'proclaim the Lord's death until he comes' (1 Cor. 11.26). It is a foretaste of the heavenly banquet, a taste of heaven on earth.

Many approaches to evangelism today have rediscovered the significance of food. It has been noticed how the meal plays this quasi-sacramental role on the Alpha course.[21] Evangelism that takes place in the context of a meal – whether around a full-blown dinner party in a home, tables in a church building, or shared snacks in a prison – places hospitality at the centre as

---

21. Richards, A., 'Eating Alpha' in *The Alpha Phenomenon: Theology, Praxis and Challenges for Mission and Church Today*, ed. Brookes, A. (London: CTBI), 330–39. For an exploration of the theological significance of Jesus' eating with 'sinners', see Blomberg, C. L., *Contagious Holiness: Jesus' Meals with Sinners* (Downers Grove: IVP, 2005).

we have seen, yet it also does something more. It is significant
that the one liturgical act that Jesus left for his followers to
engage in regularly was to eat a meal together in his own risen
presence. The early church expression of this might well have
been what we often call the 'Agape' – an occasion where the
church sat down for a normal meal, with normal food and
drink, and during which part of the bread and the wine shared
in the meal was prayed over and set aside as denoting in
some way the body and blood of Christ to be shared together.
It is claiming too much to suggest that the meal on Alpha is
in any way equivalent to the Eucharist; however, the nature
of the 'Agape' meal does narrow the gap between our usual
experience of formal Holy Communion in church and the
informality of an Alpha meal, or in the words of Anne Richards,
it 'foreshadows the full sacramental life of participating in the
Holy Communion within the fellowship of the church.'[22]

The Eucharist has its roots in the Jewish Passover. Jesus
himself often spoke of the heavenly banquet to which all
were invited. In Luke 14, the 'Parable of the Great Banquet'
starts with a fellow guest at table uttering the pious platitude:
'Blessed is the man who will eat at the feast in the kingdom of
God.' Jesus goes on to emphasise the extent of the welcome God
gives to this eschatological feast. People are invited in from the
east and west, and there is almost a sense of reckless welcome.
When the initial invitations are turned down, he changes tack:

> 'Go out quickly into the streets and alleys of the town and
> bring in the poor, the crippled, the blind and the lame.' 'Sir,' the
> servant said, 'what you ordered has been done, but there is still
> room.' Then the master told his servant, 'Go out to the roads and
> country lanes and make them come in, so that my house will be
> full.'

Luke 14.21–23

---

22. Richards, 'Eating Alpha', 337.

The chapter before has an echo of the prophetic end-time welcome to all peoples, including Gentiles, to feast with God's people in his own home: 'People will come from east and west and north and south, and will take their places at the feast in the kingdom of God' (Lk. 13.29). Jesus institutes the new Passover in that context. The Christian community, sitting down at table together, Jew and Gentile, male and female, rich and poor is intended as a small, imperfect but nonetheless real anticipation of the day when God's kingdom comes and people from all cultures and corners of the earth sit down at the heavenly banquet with God as the host. The meal on Alpha is not sacramental in the fullest sense. Yet in its indiscriminate welcome to all-comers, with faith and without faith, all in the context of the church as God's people, and in its very informality as a full meal with the purpose of finding Christ together, it can play this eschatological, anticipatory role.

Evangelistic processes need to entice, beguile and beckon. They need to offer the promise of something more, the tantalising glimpse of something yet to come, yet which is touched here and now. As well as pointing backward to the work of Christ in the past, they need to point forward to life in the Spirit. One way of including this sense of anticipation is offering prayer for healing as part of a process of evangelism. This of course touches on an ancient Christian conviction that the church relies not only on medical means for the healing of our bodies, but also prays for healing as an anticipation of the resurrection body that is promised to those who are in Christ. Christian healing is always eschatological in that sense: it is real, but always incomplete, temporary and partial. It does not stave off the inevitability of death, but it sets up a marker in the present that God can and does overcome sickness, death and hell. To see people experiencing even partial healing is a powerful way to grasp the dynamic of the gospel – the real experience in the present of the kingdom that will one day come, a reassurance of the love and compassion of God in ordinary, physical bodies – that he cares when we hurt. Putting

prayer for healing in a course on basic Christianity states this
sense of anticipation dramatically and vividly.[23]

Evangelism as anticipation gives a sense that there is more
to come. It gives a taste, often a literal taste of what the future
might hold. It models the Christian life as a life of hope, looking
for the new heavens and the new earth, the day when creation
will be renewed and 'people will come from east and west and
north and south, and will take their places at the feast in the
kingdom of God.'[24]

23. Sheils, W. J., Ed., *The Church and Healing* (Studies in Church History, Oxford: Basil Blackwell, 1982), published for the Ecclesiastical History Society, shows the extensive evidence for prayer for healing, both medical and miraculous, as a standard form of Christian ministry for centuries and throughout virtually every Christian tradition.
24. Lk. 13.29.

CHAPTER 6

THE HOLY SPIRIT
AND THE WORLD

The great South African missiologist David Bosch wrote in his magisterial book on Christian mission: 'Evangelism is ... a call to service ... . Evangelism is calling people to Mission.'[1] The purpose of evangelism is not just the conversion of individuals, nor even the growth and enlargement of the church, it is nothing less than inviting people to fulfil their fundamental human calling to join in the mission of God to heal, restore and renew the world.

The last chapter looked at a style of evangelism that takes seriously a theology of the Holy Spirit, and in particular how a new identity can be found through a catechetical process involving Christian hospitality and encounter with God, along with a sense of promise and anticipation of the future. This chapter focuses on the other side of the two main themes we have been exploring: vocation, or calling. When the Spirit unites us with Christ, so that we know the love of the Father, this also gives a new sense of purpose to human life – to play our part in the work of God through the Spirit in the renewal, healing and completion of creation. As the Spirit unites us with Christ so that we know the love of the Father, we begin to experience not just the same relationship Jesus had with the Father, but also the same relationship he had with the world. This chapter digs

---

1. Bosch, D. J., *Transforming Mission: Paradigm Shifts in Theology of Mission* (Maryknoll, New York: Orbis Books, 1991), 418.

a little deeper into this new vocation, our human calling, takes a look at how the Holy Spirit is at work healing and renewing creation and how we can play a part in that, looking forward to the day when God will bring in his kingdom.

Out of all the 'spiritualities' on offer today, only a robust theology of the Holy Spirit, as opposed to notions of secular 'spirituality', offers true, profound transformation. Michael Welker contrasts a Christian understanding of the Holy Spirit with the idea of 'spirit' found in both Aristotle and Hegel. Aristotle's understanding of spirit is really 'the activity of thinking'.[2] For Aristotle, 'spirit' is reduced to rationality. Joy and life are simply a matter of intellectual pleasure. This is akin to the 'Dawkins spirituality' – the rationalist approach that finds meaning only in what can be scientifically proven. Hegel's understanding of spirit goes further than that, to understand it as 'the true and complete principle of community'[3] – the *Geist'* or common animating force of a particular group of people. For Hegel, that spirit is something they all share in common – not something outside of themselves that draws them into another world or style of life, but something they happen to have in common, a bit like a shared love for cars, sailing or politics.

The problem with both views of spirit, according to Welker, is that neither can really change anything: 'It is impossible to see how this spirit could be a power for change, reversal and new beginning ...'[4] Hegel may be a more communal improvement on individualist Aristotelian rationalist metaphysics, but in the end, even Hegelian pneumatology remains 'simplistic and barren.'[5]

Instead he suggests, the Holy Spirit offers radical transformation – a genuinely new identity and a new purpose. The Spirit changes people in that they are 'so powerfully enlisted, that they ... orient themselves to acting for the benefit of others. The Spirit of God effects a domain of liberation and of freedom.' The Holy Spirit is not just a mood or aura we all share

2. Welker, M., *God the Spirit* (Minneapolis: Fortress, 1994), 286.
3. *Ibid.*, 292.
4. *Ibid.*, 294.
5. *Ibid.*, 295.

in common – it is a definite realm into which we are drawn
outside ourselves, with a different agenda, mode of operation
and motivation. It changes us into new people, and gives us a
new set of priorities and goals.

The Spirit Transforming the World

Few Christians would argue that Christian faith has little to
say about society or even desire to impact upon it, yet how
far can we say that it is the church's task to transform society?
There is a strong Christian ethical tradition that suggests this
is a distraction from the church's main focus. In one version of
this view, the ultimate question of the destiny of individuals
to heaven or hell must take priority over social transformation
because of the urgency of judgement. Eternity must matter
more than temporal amelioration of social conditions, because
this world is destined for destruction, while souls last for
ever in eternal life or damnation. The difficulty here is the
questionable eschatology. Is the creation really to be consigned
to the scrapheap, as a failed experiment on God's part? A
biblical eschatology would suggest that the goal of history is
the renewal of creation, a new heaven and a new earth (2 Pet.
3.13 etc.), the kingdom coming on earth as it is in heaven, not
vice versa. If so, surely Christians have an interest in the future
of creation, including its non-human dimensions. There is, as
we have seen earlier in this book, a mandate in Jesus' teaching
on the kingdom of God, for at least some contribution of the
church to the society and community around it.
   A different and more sophisticated version of the critique
comes from the broadly Anabaptist tradition, whose best
known advocate is Stanley Hauerwas, the American ethical
theologian. He argues that the church has no interest in shoring
up a world that is determined to live without God. The role of
the church is not to try to make the world a better place, but
to bear witness to the fact that God has made possible a new

world.[6] The ultimate reality is the kingdom of God, embodied in Jesus. The goal of history is the kingdom, not a patched-up version of humanist social democracy, so the church needs to put all its energy into bearing witness to that kingdom in its own life, becoming a community of 'resident aliens' within the world, rather than trying to build a just social order.[7]

Although he can sound like it, Hauerwas does not in fact promote the idea that Christians should shun social life and have nothing to say to the world outside its doors. The church plays a vital role in liberal societies. For him, the project of liberal societies is to attempt to 'make a just society without just people',[8] echoing T.S. Eliot's charge that modern societies are always 'dreaming of systems so perfect that no one will need to be good.'[9]

The church, however, plays the vital role of a community with the ability to produce people of character and virtue: 'the most important social task of Christians is to be nothing less than a community capable of forming people with virtues sufficient to witness to God's truth in the world.'[10] Or, to put it in other terms: 'insofar as the church can reclaim its integrity as a community of virtue, it can be of great service in liberal societies.'[11] In fact, 'the most important service the church does for any society is to be a community capable of developing people of virtue.'[12]

As we saw in chapter four, despite the lack of a developed theology of the Spirit, Hauerwas' main point is well made. The church is oriented fundamentally towards the kingdom of God, as an anticipation of the new creation, rather than having as its central task the amelioration of bankrupt social systems. The church is not a piece of sticking plaster for a broken world, it is

6. Hauerwas, S., *A Community of Character: Toward a Constructive Christian Social Ethic* (Notre Dame: University of Notre Dame Press, 1981).
7. Hauerwas, S. and Willimon, W. H., *Resident Aliens: Life in the Christian Colony* (Nashville: Abingdon Press, 1989).
8. Hauerwas, S. and Pinches, C., *Christians Among the Virtues: Theological Conversations with Ancient and Modern Ethics* (Notre Dame: University of Notre Dame Press, 1997), 149.
9. Eliot, T. S., *Choruses from 'The Rock'*, VI.
10. Hauerwas, A *Community of Character Ethic*, 3.
11. Hauerwas, S., *Vision and Virtue: Essays in Christian Ethical Reflection*, 7.
12. *Ibid.*, 13.

a sign pointing to a different order altogether. If this is so, how then does it relate to this new creation, while it lives in exile within a world that forgets God? There are perhaps three ways in which this relationship between the church, the kingdom of God and society can be expressed.

Church, Kingdom and Society

First, the church *bears witness* to the kingdom. It points forward to the coming of the kingdom, the day of resurrection, in its proclamation and witness. Through what it says and what it does, it reminds the rest of the world that either forgets, or doesn't really believe that any other world is possible than this broken, badly functioning and unjust order, that a new day is coming when God will renew the creation and destroy evil once and for all. The church preaches and announces the imminent arrival of a new creation – that there is hope. Fully to bear witness to this reality, it also engages with the various communities around it, erecting signs of the coming kingdom, changing social realities where it can so that it reflects something and reminds people of that kingdom.

Second, the church not only points forward, but actually *embodies* the new creation and gives a genuine foretaste of it. As we have already seen, this is the significance of the experience of the love and power of God made available through the Holy Spirit, the downpayment of the age to come. It also comes about in the church's own life. The church is called to be an anticipation of the new creation, a kind of sacramental sign of the kingdom that is to come.[13]

The third way in which the church relates to the new creation is that (in the words of N.T. Wright)[14] it *builds for* that kingdom. Through the power of the Spirit, the church's involvement with social transformation always has an eschatological focus – it seeks to engage in social problems

---

13. For a development of this point, see Tomlin, G., *The Provocative Church* (London: SPCK, 2002), Ch. 4.
14. Wright, N. T., *Surprised by Hope* (London: SPCK, 2007), 263.

such as homelessness, family breakdown, the dehumanising of
work practices and the like, out of a conviction that this world
is destined for something better, and that in some way, what we
do now will, in the providence of God, not be lost, but be built
into that new creation.[15] St Paul writes of how Christians need
to watch carefully how they live, or build on the foundation of
Christ (to use his own metaphor) in this age. What they build
needs to be such that it will survive the fire of judgement.
The implication is that what we build now can last into the
new creation; acts and projects of compassion, humility and
generosity will somehow be incorporated into the new order of
things:

> ... each one should be careful how he builds. For no one can lay
> any foundation other than the one already laid, which is Jesus
> Christ. If any man builds on this foundation using gold, silver,
> costly stones, wood, hay or straw, his work will be shown for
> what it is, because the Day will bring it to light. It will be revealed
> with fire, and the fire will test the quality of each man's work.
> If what he has built survives, he will receive his reward. If it is
> burned up, he will suffer loss; he himself will be saved, but only
> as one escaping through the flames.

I Corinthians 3.10–15

By the Holy Spirit who brings creation to its fulfilment (and
again we are taking seriously the empowering of the Spirit as
an actual experienced reality, not just a nod in this direction
for theological correctness), Christians find a new desire to be
involved in the transformation of society, to see it reflect more
of the kingdom of God, out of these fundamental eschatological
convictions. This is precisely the work of the Spirit. The true
test of whether the Spirit is at work, is both the presence of
experiences of the numinous power of God, and the outcome of

---

15. Luke Bretherton notes the lack of a pneumatology in Hauerwas's ethics, and makes the
important point that the difference between Christian and non-Christian action in the world is not
necessarily that they do different things, but that they are oriented towards a different goal. See
Bretherton, L., *Hospitality as Holiness: Christian Witness amid Moral Diversity*, 115.

those experiences in people becoming agents of change in the
world. As Clark Pinnock puts it: 'It is God that gives the world
a future, and the Spirit that brings it to pass.'[16]
  The goal of such involvement is not to 'make the world a
better place' for its own sake, so that one day it might somehow
evolve into the kingdom of God, as if by the church's efforts
and the work of all people of good will we can somehow
build the kingdom of God on earth. Instead Christian social
action waits patiently for God's action in bringing about the
new creation, yet builds for it in the present, knowing that its
labours are not in vain (1 Cor. 15.58). The church bears witness
to, anticipates and builds for the coming kingdom. It is in this
sense that Jeremiah's advice to the Israelite exiles works:

> Build houses and settle down; plant gardens and eat what they
> produce. Marry and have sons and daughters; find wives for
> your sons and give your daughters in marriage, so that they too
> may have sons and daughters. Increase in number there; do not
> decrease. Also, seek the peace and prosperity of the city to which
> I have carried you into exile. Pray to the Lord for it, because if it
> prospers, you too will prosper.
>
> **Jeremiah 29.5–7**

Although in the deepest sense they are in exile, longing for
home, they are to seek the welfare of their place of exile because
God will one day bring them to their true home where he will
reign. What they build in exile will in some way contribute to
the future – the welfare of the secular city is in a profound way
bound up with the future coming of the kingdom.

The Arenas of the Spirit's Action

We might be tempted to think of the church as the main arena
of life in the Spirit. However, if we are thinking of the prodigal

---

16. Pinnock, C., *Flame of Love: A Theology of the Holy Spirit*, 70.

Spirit, proceeding from the Father through the Son to draw creation back into the love of God, we need to learn to expand our vision and look wider to find the Spirit's realm of activity. The prodigal Spirit travels far beyond the doors of the church, seeking out lost creation to entice and accompany it back along the path blazed by the divine Son of God. If the Spirit is healing and bringing creation to its fulfilment, then creation is the arena of the Spirit's work, rather than just the church. This happens in at least three ways. First, the Spirit is the author of life – he gives life to all things, as the animating principle of the world. Second (and this is a function of the Spirit after the fall), he is at work in the world bringing life out of death, overcoming the powers that would drag the world back into chaos and leading it towards its proper fulfilment. Third, he gives new identity and calling to humankind, so that we can be recalled to our true vocation as humanity remade in the image of God, watching and working with him towards the new creation.

We will look at the church, and what it needs to be to engage in this mission in the next chapter. First, however, we take four areas of the Spirit's work in the world: the arenas of work, family, community and the environment, to explore how a theology focused on the Spirit helps us see each one of these transformed.

Work

In the second creation story in Genesis 2, we find a rich pneumatology of work. When God initially creates the world, it is barren and dry:

> When the Lord God made the earth and the heavens – and no shrub of the field had yet appeared on the earth and no plant of the field had yet sprung up, for the Lord God had not sent rain on the earth and there was no man to work the ground.

Genesis 2.4–5

Without human presence and work, the earth remains empty and desolate. Then God does two things: he sends water – 'streams came up from the earth and watered the whole surface of the ground' (v.6) – and he creates humankind through his breath: 'The Lord God formed the man from the dust of the ground, and breathed into his nostrils the breath of life, and the man became a living being' (v.7).

Both water and breath are of course common images in Scripture for the Holy Spirit. It is too much to claim that the author was consciously using these as metaphors for the Spirit, but in the light of the rest of Scripture, we can see these two actions of God, drawing water from the earth, and breathing life into human bodies, as acts more particularly associated with the Holy Spirit. Adam is given identity (created and given life by God) and he is now given a task: 'The Lord God took the man and put him in the Garden of Eden to work it and take care of it.' God then brings the animals to the man and asks him to name them. God presumably could have named them himself and informed humankind what they were, but he invites the man instead to give order, shape and structure to the world, to describe it in human language. When woman is created, she is described as a 'helper' – the focus is on her as a co-worker with the man, sharing equally in the task of working and taking care of the particular part of the earth in which they are placed.

In this deceptively brief story we find all the elements of human work. There is physical agricultural work, bringing fruit and produce from the land. There is scientific work, analysing, understanding and distinguishing between the different parts of creation. There is artistic work, expressing reality in language and form. The first creation story in Genesis 1 contains the instruction to 'fill the earth and subdue it' (1.28). Picture a garden of unruly growth, plants and grass growing wild and uncontrolled. Humanity has the task to bring order and beauty out of the life that God has given.

Through human work, the fertile life given by the Spirit of God is given order and beauty. It is harnessed so it works for the good of the whole of creation, and for its proper development, so that its full potential can be realised. Wheat is turned into bread. Water and grapes are turned into wine. Stone and wood are turned into homes. Electricity is turned into light.

Humanity is created 'from the dust of the ground' emphasising the sense that we are rooted in the earth itself, made out of the same stuff as the rest of creation. We are not lifted above it, made out of some magical stardust. We belong to the earth as every funeral service says: dust to dust, ashes to ashes. In one sense we are animals like all the others. At the same time, however, humanity is chosen out of all the animal species created on the earth to play a special role of mediating the presence and care of God to the rest of creation. Humanity is both from the earth *and* made in God's image. That role is to enable creation to praise God as it should. And this is the work of the Spirit. The Spirit fills Bezalel, son of Uri, to make artistic designs for the Temple (Ex. 31.2–5), taking gold, silver and bronze, stones and wood to make something that is full of beauty and which praises God. Such artistic or technological work is performed through the Spirit, because the Spirit is the one who draws creation into the sphere of the love of God so that people are enabled to become what they have the potential to be.

Human work takes the various parts of creation and re-imagines or combines them into new patterns to enable them to glorify the creator. That may be the minerals of the earth shaped by technology into mobile phones, park benches or trains. It may be paint or bronze moulded into art or sculpture. It may be prudent financial management to create wealth. It might be forestry that enables trees to grow as trees should. If the natural world praises God most fully by being itself, as suggested by the Psalms that envisage the trees of the fields clapping their hands and the mountains skipping for joy in the presence of God, then human activity to preserve or fulfil the proper potential of nature is part of our vocation to enable creation to glorify its creator. Human work enables the rest of creation, both human and non-human to fulfil its potential, to grow towards the new creation. Work has to be seen in eschatological context.

Yet of course not all work feels that way. A lot of work is experienced as drudgery, just a means of earning enough to get drunk at the weekend, go on exotic holidays to escape the boredom of labour, or simply to accumulate wealth for personal pleasure. So work needs to be redeemed. Work or art that dehumanises or alienates, that misleads about God or other people, that cheats others out of what God has given them, in other words, work that does not enable the creation to praise its creator, is work outside the Spirit. After the fall, the Spirit plays another role – to heal and renew humanity so it is able to play the part of not just developing an incomplete creation, but healing a damaged one. That is where other aspects of human work enter the stage: medical science to cure sickness, legal or police work to ensure justice, or ecological care to eradicate environmental destruction. We have, as Miroslav Volf argues, a responsibility to find work that is fulfilling and builds for the kingdom of God.[17]

When we can imagine our work being taken up by the Spirit to build the new creation, it brings a new dignity and focus to work. The New Testament sees work in an eschatological context: 'Whatever you do, work at it with all your heart, as working for the Lord, not for men, since you know that you will receive an inheritance from the Lord as a reward. It is the Lord Christ you are serving.'[18] Work in the Spirit is not performed for monetary reward or human acclamation – it is done in and for Christ. It is an offering of praise and a contribution towards the day when all things in heaven and earth, including the product of our honest prayerful work, will be brought together under Christ.

Human work, far from a distraction from the realm of the Spirit, is in fact right at its heart, the arena where we exercise our divinely-given vocation in harmony with the Spirit of

---

17. Volf, M., *Work in the Spirit: Towards a Theology of Work* (New York: Oxford University Press, 1991).
18. Col. 3.23f.

God. A church that is sensitive to this dimension will not so much expect lay people to pray for and support the work of the church (as if that is the primary arena of the Spirit's work), but ensure the church prays for and supports the activity and involvement of its people in the workplace.

Family

The second arena of the Spirit is the realm of the family. In classic Christian theology, marriage and family are ordinances of creation not redemption. In other words they are good for all human life, Christian and otherwise. Pope John Paul II's Apostolic Exhortation of 1992, *Familiaris Consortio*, pointed to the vital link between the family, society and public virtue.

> The family has vital and organic links with society, since it is its foundation and nourishes it continually through its role of service to life: it is from the family that citizens come to birth and it is within the family that they find the first school of the social virtues that are the animating principle of the existence and development of society itself.[19]

John Paul's *Letter to Families* of 1994 takes this further by arguing that the family was central to the 'civilisation of love', the ideal of a culture permeated by Christian witness and presence: 'The family is a community of persons and the smallest social unit. As such it is an *institution* fundamental to the life of every society.'[20] Strong family life is a central part of witness to the kingdom of God, the place where God has his way. Addressing the quality and hence the stability of marriage and family life is therefore a crucial task in bearing witness to the will and intention of God in the world. It is, in the words of John Paul II, an 'inescapable requirement of the work of evangelisation'. If the heart of reality is the love between Father

19. 'Familiaris Consortio', accessed September 3, 2010, http://www.vatican.va/holy_father/john_paul_ii/apost_exhortations/documents/hf_jp-ii_exh_19811122_familiaris-consortio_en.html.
20. 'Letter to families from Pope John Paul II', accessed September 3, 2010, http://www.vatican.va/holy_father/john_paul_ii/letters/documents/hf_jp-ii_let_02021994_families_en.html.

and Son, into which we are invited by the Spirit, then enabling healthy relationships lies at the very centre of Christian ministry and witness.

Alongside St Augustine's very influential idea that the Spirit is the bond of love between the Father and Son, there was another important tradition of Trinitarian thought in the Middle Ages, originating from the Scottish theologian Richard of St Victor (d. 1183) and continuing through Franciscan theologians such as Bonaventure. In this approach, rather than identifying the Spirit as the love between the Father and the Son, the focus is on love as the very nature of God. For God to be love, argues Richard, he cannot be alone: love needs an object that is worthy of that love. Moreover, if that divine love is to be complete, God has to be more than just Father and Son, because binary love is self-enclosed. True love always finds or begets another to be the object of the love shared between the two. A love that consists merely of two people gazing into each other's eyes is fruitless and in the end a little annoying. Love must be self-transcending, welcoming others into that love. Therefore, argues Richard, there must be a *third* person in the Trinity for God to be truly *love*, rather than just *loving*.[21] 'In order for charity to be true, it requires a plurality of persons, in order for charity to be perfected, it requires a Trinity of persons.'[22]

This gives a Trinitarian theological rationale for family life. We live in a culture that idolises romantic love. Love that is self-enclosed, or even sex which is solely about pleasure or conquest, is limited and stunted. True love between two people always seeks to move out from itself to embrace others, whether that means children born within the security of a committed, secure long-term relationship of love (just as in Richard's theology, the Spirit proceeds from the eternal love between the Father and the Son), or to friends and strangers who are welcomed into a home, and embraced within the love of the hosts. This also offers a model of relationships for single people

---

21. See the helpful summary of the Trinitarian theology of Richard of St Victor in Burgess, S. M., *The Holy Spirit: Medieval Roman Catholic and Reformation Traditions.* (Peabody Mass: Hendricksen, 1997), 63–69.
22. Richard of St Victor, *De Trinitate*, III.xiii.

as well: singleness is not to be a reason for isolation or defensive privacy, but an opportunity to develop intimate and close friendships, which themselves can be the source of extending love to the stranger.

If the Spirit welcomes us into the love of the Father and the Son, a love in which we find our true identity and vocation, that can give us a picture of how human families are to work. They are to be places of love where children can discover their own identity and vocation. That means life in the Spirit means paying close attention to the quality of the relationships between husband and wife. When love in marriage is allowed to die, children often become uncertain of who they are. Are they loved? The father or mother who abandons the family so often leaves behind children suddenly unsure of their value or place in the world. Divorce erodes both identity and vocation.

As we grow up, families are the places where we are formed and shaped. Parents are the first mediators of the love and grace of God to us in our early years. Children are to obey their parents 'in the Lord' (Eph. 6.1), because in a way parents represent God to children – they are called to be mediators of God's love and discipline. So family, like work, is one of the ways in which God's love and care for the world are expressed within the world. If families play this role in forming and shaping us, this is so obviously the work of the Spirit that they must be one of the central arenas for the work of the Spirit in the world – enabling children to become what they have the potential to be. Like work, not all family life expresses that love properly. Families can be damaging and unhealthy, just as work can be dehumanising and dull. That is why there can be fewer higher priorities for a church that lives in the Spirit, than seeking to become communities where the success and longevity of marriage, both Christian and non-Christian, is taught, enabled and promoted.

Churches are meant to be communities that help people learn what it means to love someone else, whether a spouse, a child or a parent. Dallas Willard writes of how local churches need to take the process of spiritual formation much more seriously than they do. They need to become 'academies of life' in which the vital skills of harmonious and godly living are taught and learnt.[23] Families are where we learn these skills (or don't learn them), and for that reason, churches need to invest heavily in resourcing families.

Naturally, the Trinity is not exclusively a model for family life. It can also provide a rationale for deep friendship. In Aelred of Rievaulx's classic *Spiritual Friendship*, human friendship at its best is marked by the same kind of mutual attentiveness, intimacy and self-giving that we find between Father, Son and Holy Spirit, and flourishes best in mutual fellowship with God in Christ. Families matter because they are the primary context in which children are formed and grow into healthy or unhealthy adults. Nonetheless friendship can equally reflect the ideal of human relationship that we find in the Trinity. Like family, good friendship is close but not exclusive. It binds tightly, but not in such a way that it refuses to allow others to share in it. Such open friendship can both express the life of God and be a window into experiencing that divine life.[24]

Politics

The third arena in which human life is lived is that of politics or government. This does not just mean national party politics, but more the life of the *polis* – the city, the town, the village. In other words it refers to the quality of life that we live together beyond the immediate bonds of family life. It involves local government, the oversight of the economy, the legal and penal systems, social inclusion, shelter, community cohesion and many more. If the Spirit is at work to draw creation to its fulfilment and if this involves the taking up of the life of the kingdom here in the present into the coming day of resurrection, then this arena, the life of wider local communities surrounding church communities is one of the arenas of the

23. Willard, D., *The Spirit of the Disciplines: Understanding How God Changes Lives* (London: Hodder & Stoughton, 1988), xiv.
24. Aelred of Rievaulx, *Spiritual Friendship* (Kalamazoo: Cistercian Publications, 1974).

Spirit's action. For effective witness to and embodiment of the kingdom of God, the church has a stake in enabling people to find a social order that reflects something of the will and intention of God.

The Spirit anoints Jesus to preach good news to the poor, to bring freedom for the prisoners, recovery of sight for the blind, and to release the oppressed.[25] One of the signs of the Spirit's work is precisely this passionate concern that those far from the love of God might be brought back to experience the self-giving compassion, welcome and embrace of the Father for the Son. Charlie Mackesy's sculpture of the prodigal embraced by the Father, which might also be seen as a picture of God the Father's love for God the Son, is also a picture of the love of God for the excluded and the unloved.

As we have seen, the gospel is an act of hospitality, where the Spirit invites us and a broken world into the love that beats at the heart of God, as an anticipation of the coming day when all creation will be brought to fulfilment in God's love. This model of the Spirit as the one who welcomes us hospitably into the life of God can serve as a model for understanding the Spirit's work and our involvement in it, in the context of local community life.

Recent writing on political theology has explored the value of the idea of hospitality as a very productive concept for Christian engagement with a pluralist multi-faith society. Luke Bretherton writes of a kind of 'hospitable politics', where the church takes a lead in generating common action in a community, but involves others in that action, which works alongside a 'politics of the common good' where Christians work with non-Christians seeking the welfare of the city together on more neutral ground.[26] As the Spirit welcomes us back into fellowship with God, establishing relationship where there was none before, bringing into lived experience the forgiveness and grace that flows through the cross of the incarnate Son, so Christians and churches that are touched

25. Lk. 4.18.
26. Bretherton, L., *Christianity and Contemporary Politics: The Conditions and Possibilities of Faithful Witness* (Chichester: Wiley-Blackwell, 2010), 219f. See also Bretherton, *Hospitality as Holiness*.

by this same Spirit will find themselves doing something similar in their local communities. They will start to welcome the homeless, the excluded and those normally disdained in some way, and to begin relationship with them, as an echo of the same hospitality that God extends to them, and as an anticipation of the future order when all things will be brought together under Christ.

This might mean long-term drop-in centres that use church buildings for acts of hospitality. This goes beyond handouts or the donation of clothes or money that can encourage a patronising dependency. Instead it establishes relationship in a prophetic way, especially when it cuts across the normal kinds of relationships that operate in a particular local community. It might mean working together with other faith groups or community bodies to seek fair rents, or against unjust loan arrangements that entrap poorer people into long-term dependency. The Spirit who draws us into the love of God enables us to find a new identity and purpose, leading to new liberty and healing. These relationships between Christians and others, established in the arena of the *polis*, will do the same thing. Rather than perpetuating dependency, the act of welcome that gives the neighbour or the stranger the space to tell their story, to be treated as the beloved creation of God, enables them also to find a new identity and purpose, even things as practical and real as new homes, jobs or direction.

When the homeless find a welcome in the name of Christ, when those in debt find that debt cancelled or redeemed, when work becomes fulfilling and fruitful, when an ex-prisoner turns from crime to find gainful employment, when a couple decide not to get divorced but find the resources to rebuild their marriage, that is the work of the Holy Spirit of life, the kingdom coming in power, people being touched by the healing love of God. These become visible, tangible foretastes, anticipations, building blocks of the new creation, where they will be the norm not the exception. In a very real sense this is integral to the ministry of the Holy Spirit – that people's lives may be turned away from trivialities like chasing after money, sex, power and fame, and instead become involved in the greatest and most fulfilling of all vocations: building for the kingdom of God.

The church exists not for its own sake, but so that it can call humanity back to its proper task to work with God for the healing and renewal of creation. The point of church growth is to draw people back into relationships with God in Christ through the Spirit, to facilitate the mission of God in the world. To make church growth the defining purpose of the church is to confuse a means for an end. The real reason churches need to grow is so they can provide a faithful witness to the kingdom of God, and build effectively and fruitfully for that coming kingdom.

On the one hand, churches that are embarrassed about evangelism will eventually dry up, with fewer and fewer people doing more and more (or in fact, less and less), and with little sense of the ever-present dynamic power of God to change people and situations. Churches that only do evangelism miss the point of evangelism, which is to draw people into the love of God, so they might be cleansed, transformed and capable of fulfilling the true human calling: to care for creation and help to bring it to its fulfillment in Christ. Hospitality is the key to both: the hospitality of the Spirit who welcomes us into the dynamic and liberating love of God.

The Environment

The last arena of the Spirit's work in the world is that of the natural world, the environment that we inhabit. Recent years have seen the environment become one of the hottest political topics around, one which no politician can be seen to ignore. Does Christian faith have anything to add to contemporary anxieties about climate change, the destruction of ecosystems and the extinction of species? The understanding we have been developing of humanity's role alongside the Spirit in the care and growth of the created order adds something significant to this debate.

First, it places it close to the heart of any Christian agenda for the modern world. This is far from a distraction from more spiritual concerns: it is a deeply Christian issue because it is a deeply human calling. If humanity is called to work and take care of creation, then Christians, true to their calling to be the new humanity in Christ, are to embrace this fully as a high priority in any local engagement.

Second, a pneumatologically-focused Christian faith is the only realistic grounding for believing that the earth needs to be preserved.[27] Ancient views of nature were various. The cosmology found in the various Babylonian and Greek myths of creation (against which the book of Genesis offers a conscious contrast) saw the world as the result of fallout from warfare in the divine courts – it is an accidental by-product of the violence of the gods, hardly a strong basis on which to argue for its value and intrinsic worth. The Greek epics of Homer and Hesiod saw the world as changing, but doing so negatively. The world is degenerating from its original age of gold and there is next to nothing we can do about it. Plato saw the physical world as an imperfect copy of what really mattered: abstract 'forms' that existed in changeless perfection on some metaphysical plane above us. First-century Gnostics, in a strange mythological version of Plato's view of the world, thought our destiny and goal must therefore be to escape this ugly and flawed place to the realm of pure spirit.

In other words, none of these really saw the physical world as inherently *good*, and therefore worth preserving. They were either mired in a gloomy pessimism about the future, or their optimism was based on escaping the physical universe to enter a spiritual world elsewhere. Neither approach gives a robust basis for action to preserve the earth. More modern views fare little better. Contemporary scientific atheism is forced to admit that the world came about essentially by accident. It can have

---

27. I am indebted to an unpublished paper by James Orr for some of the insights in the following paragraphs: 'The Creation Crunch: Theological and Philosophical Perspectives on Climate Change' (March 2009).

no intrinsic meaning or value other than that which we choose to give it. There may be a set of physical laws that shape its emergence, or biological patterns that govern the evolution of life, but its origin lies in meaningless randomness and chance.

Now it is unquestioned dogma today that the earth needs to be preserved. Climate change is perhaps the greatest threat facing not just human life but life itself on the planet, and no one doubts the need to preserve the black rhino, the baobab tree and the Baltic Sea. When it comes to answering the question of *why* such things are worth preserving, the answers get a little thin. Usually some kind of pragmatic reason is given. The most commonly cited reason is survival: we need to preserve the earth for our grandchildren. But isn't that just another instrumental reason that suggests creation exists for our benefit rather than being good in itself? It assumes survival is the greatest good, but it still doesn't give any meaning to that survival or any value to the world. Surely life is more than mere survival? Secular humanism, which has to conclude that there is no ultimate meaning, purpose or value intrinsic to the physical world, surely leads to the rather lame conclusion that the only reason we value the earth is because it is the only place we have to live on and we don't want to die. The idea that the earth needs preserving because it is the only home we have is just the kind of anthropocentric view of the world that many environmentalists think got us into this mess in the first place. Doesn't it fail to answer the question?

In contrast to all of these, only the Judeo-Christian doctrine of creation says that the physical world around us is fundamentally and irrevocably *good*. This planet is a good thing in itself. It doesn't require human life to make it good, because its goodness is derived from its origins in the love of a good and creative God, the one who looked at and pronounced it good, once and for all (Gn. 1.31). Moreover it has a future. The Spirit breathes life into dead forms, and draws creation onto its destiny. Only this view gives a thorough grounding for modern ecological concern, giving the universe a value in itself, and a future to hope for. It is worth preserving because it is a good thing. Not because we feel sorry for our descendants, not because we need a place to live, but just because, to quote L'Oréal, it is worth it.

The Spirit broods over creation, fulfils and perfects it. And he does that because creation is a good thing. God enlists the help of humanity to mediate his love and creative presence to the world, and when humans became part of the problem rather than part of the solution, he sends his Son to redeem us and his Spirit to fill us so that we can be restored to fellowship with him and play our proper role in the world all over again.

Third, we are not alone in our attempts to save the planet. Much green rhetoric places a large heap of guilt on people as consumers, implying that it is entirely up to us whether the planet is rescued or gradually (or suddenly) implodes. As we survey a creation 'in bondage to decay' (Rom. 8.21), the Spirit 'helps us in our weakness' (v.26). The Spirit is at work within creation, constantly renewing it, giving it life, overcoming decay, bringing life where there is death, growing blades of grass through the ageing concrete of the bleak urban landscape. There is hope amidst environmental destruction, not because humanity is finally on the case, but because when we do recover our original, divinely-given task of caring for creation, harnessing it so it can become what it was created to be, we are joining in a work which the Spirit of God has been doing since the dawn of the age. We are working with the grain of life, walking in step with the Spirit[28] who broods over creation and brings it to completion.

Intercession

There is one further dimension of the church's involvement in the world that we have not yet properly examined, and that is the place of prayer. Prayer in the Spirit involves being invited by the Spirit into the divine conversation at the heart of the

---

28. Gal. 5.25.

Trinity.[29] However, it is particularly intercessory prayer that raises issues for a theology of the Spirit in the context of the world.[30] All Christian prayer takes its cue from the prayer Jesus taught his disciples to pray, and at the heart of that prayer lies the petition: 'Your kingdom come, on earth as it is in heaven.' This expresses a longing for things to be different, for God to act.

Jesus places intercessory prayer as a high priority for his followers. Yet it can pose a theological difficulty – the Lord's Prayer is embarrassingly full of petitions. In a psychotherapeutic age, we more easily accept the idea that prayer can change us than how it can change the world. Meditation and contemplation are more easily accommodated in a world where they fit quite happily into other religious and spiritual schemes. Intercessory prayer, however, is awkward and different. If God knows everything why do we need to pray? Surely he can act without us praying? And why does he not more frequently answer the desperate cries of his people?[31]

The theology of intercessory prayer has to be part of a wider theology of the mediation of God's work in the world. Rather than rule his creation directly, God chooses to mediate his presence through human agency. He delegates oversight, care or rule to humankind, made in his image, created to reflect his nature and will within the created order. Humans are therefore called to work the land, to bring out its potential for fruitfulness and growth, to provide for the development of life, to procreate and fill the earth. God's love for the world is therefore mediated through human agency. That is not to say it cannot be experienced directly, but even then it usually comes through created things. God presents himself and his grace to us in such things as a parent's love, a friend's word of encouragement, an enemy's act of kindness, a stunning view,

29. Pinnock, *Flame of Love*, 46.
30. Gary Badcock perceptively identifies what for him lies at the heart of the charismatic contribution to global Christianity: 'at its centre stands a new depth of prayer rather than the sensational experience of the gifts of the Spirit in and for themselves.' Badcock, G. D., *Light of Truth and Fire of Love: A Theology of the Holy Spirit* (Grand Rapids: Eerdmans, 1997), 137.
31. The dilemma of God's silence in unanswered intercessory prayer is addressed in Greig, P., *God on Mute: Engaging the Silence of Unanswered Prayer* (Eastbourne: Kingsway, 2007).

and more specifically in the words of Scripture, the bread and wine of Holy Communion and the water of Baptism. Yet God's rule over the world is exercised not just through human action. It also involves human prayer. Just as God acts through human agency, he also acts through human prayer. As Kallistos Ware puts it: 'without God's grace we *can* do nothing; but without our voluntary co-operation, God *will* do nothing.'[32] It is as if he often waits for us to pray before he acts, because he wants to involve us in the process of the work of his kingdom. Human prayer takes its place alongside human work, procreation and evangelism, as the means through which God enacts his will in the world. To cry out to God in prayer is to join with him, to co-operate with him in the work of the completion of creation.

Prayer therefore is another means, alongside work and mission, of co-creation with God. God invites us to participate in his ongoing creation and his work for new creation through our prayers. Paul Fiddes describes this as adding our prayerful persuasion to God's persuasive influence on his creation.[33] There is a sense in which we can help shape the future through what we pray for, just as we help shape the future by what we work for. St Benedict's famous dictum *laborare est orare*, to work is to pray, might also be put the other way around: to pray is to work. These two activities are closer together than we might think: prayer is a form of shaping the world every bit as much as human work. And that is why it is vital to pray with as much passion and energy as we put into our work, in the world or the church.

The stance of Christians towards the world is one where prayer takes a central place. Prayer is a reminder that it doesn't all depend on us, but that the Holy Spirit is at work alongside us and through us. The danger of an approach that emphasises the human vocation to work with God in the healing and development of creation is that we get either too confident in our own powers, or too despairing that it is too much for us.

32. Ware, K., *The Orthodox Way* (New York: St Vladimir's Seminary Press, 1982), 112. Italics his.
33. Fiddes, P. S., *Participating in God: a Pastoral Doctrine of the Trinity* (London: Darton, Longman & Todd, 2000), Ch. 4.

The practice of regular personal and communal intercession crucially impresses on us that this task is beyond me, beyond the church, beyond governments. As T.S. Eliot put it:

> The Church disowned, the tower overthrown, the bell upturned, what have we to do
> But stand with empty hands and palms turned upwards
> In an age which advances progressively backwards.[34]

This is precisely, even literally, the posture taken up by the church as it prays for change. The Spirit works through the church, but works in the world to make the world the kind of place that reflects God's wisdom and love. Through both human prayer and through human Christian action, the Spirit transforms real, ordinary, physical human life and community.

---

34. Eliot, T. S., *Choruses from 'The Rock'*, VII.

CHAPTER 7

THE HOLY SPIRIT AND THE CHURCH

A group of Christians in Washington DC got together to plant a new church. In doing so, they asked themselves some very profound and wise questions. The first was: 'What is the mission of this church?' In other words, what is it called to do? What is it here for? What is its core purpose? The second question was: 'What kind of community is needed to engage in this mission?' The third was 'what spiritual disciplines are necessary to sustain this mission?' In asking this way round, they perhaps got the order right. They began with the mission of the church, then asked about the shape that the church needed to take if it was going to be the servant of this mission, and finished with the kind of practices they needed to keep it going long term and actually make an impact, not just talk about it. Too often, churches have asked these questions the other way round – they have fixed the order and shape of the church first, usually according to ways it has been done in the past, then thought about spiritual disciplines more as a way of maintaining the pre-ordained shape of the church, and then almost as an afterthought, given some fleeting attention to the purpose or mission that church is called to (and then has often been surprised when it finds the mission bit doesn't work very well).

Getting the relationship right between missiology and ecclesiology is vital. Putting the calling of the church before its institutional character, or to put it in more formal theological terms, allowing missiology to shape ecclesiology rather than the other way round, ensures that the church retains a sense of direction and focus. It also makes the form of the church the servant of its purpose. Now of course there are limits to this. The early Fathers of the church insisted on a proper sense of continuity from age to age, so that the 'tradition' of the church was both the apostolic teaching handed down from generation to generation, and also some of the practices through which that tradition was passed on. Not everything is up for grabs. One generation is not entirely at liberty to change everything the previous generation did or used, for a very good theological reason. That reason is that although in some senses the mission of the church differs from age to age or context to context, in other ways it remains the same: to bear witness to God and the reign of Christ, in the power of the Spirit. This is what the great systematic theologies of the church have recognised. Thomas Aquinas' *Summa Theologica* starts with the nature of God and of humanity and its calling, before going on to describe the shape of human and Christian life and ending with the form of the church. Calvin's *Institutes* follow a similar pattern, starting with God as Creator and Redeemer, before thinking about the grace of Christ and how it is received, before finally looking at the nature and shape of the church as a consequence.

So there is a delicate balance to be found between continuity and change. But placing the mission of God and therefore the mission of the church before its shape and form does introduce a criterion for deciding what to preserve and what to change as the church moves from culture to culture, from age to age. This of course is where the third question comes in, about spiritual disciplines. There may be aspects of the church's previous form, spiritual disciplines and practices that aid its mission, keeping it focused on its true identity in a way that still enables those outside the church (and those inside as well!) to enter and find it intelligible and connected to life in the present. Equally, however, there may be aspects of its current practice and shape that hinder its mission and its ability to speak to and draw in those who feel estranged from it.

In these pages, we have been looking at questions of identity and calling, through the lens of a theology of the prodigal Spirit. This gives us a clear sense of human purpose: to join with the Holy Spirit in God's reaching out, his mission to the world, to bring it to its completion in Christ. The church is therefore the community especially charged in history with the role of announcing this new creation, embodying it in its own life, and being a community where people can be transformed to fulfil the purpose for which God designed them, in relationship with him. The church of course was born on the day of Pentecost. It came into being when the Spirit came upon the disciples gathered in a small upper room in Jerusalem. Christians have always recognised this. The gathering of the disciples on their own, or even with the physical presence of Jesus (they had of course met as a group together many times before) was not the church until the Spirit came. The church is constituted by the Spirit sent from the Father through the Son. When the Spirit came the church was born, and not before. As the prodigal Spirit goes out from the heart of God, seeking to draw creation back into the love of the Father for the Son, he chooses a community of people to fulfil this calling. That is why mission is so vital for an understanding of church and why mission needs to shape the form of church in any given culture. Now of course cultures change. And this is no new insight. Article 34 of the Anglican Church's *Thirty-Nine Articles of Religion* (also found in Thomas Cranmer's original 42 Articles as well) states: 'It is not necessary that Traditions and Ceremonies be in all places one and utterly like; for at all times they have been divers, and may be changed according to the diversities of countries, times and men's manners, so that nothing be ordained against God's Word.' The question is: are there markers, fixed points, guidelines that help describe what a church needs to be to fulfil the mission of the community of the Spirit, regardless of the culture in which it finds itself?

One traditional way of understanding the nature of the church has been to examine it through the lens of the four marks of the church derived from the statement in the Nicene Creed, of belief in the 'one, holy, catholic and apostolic church.' The church's identity is found in its Unity, Holiness, Catholicity and Apostolicity. Now these four characteristics can give the impression of something static, fixed, immoveable. Yet they come into their own when they are seen in the light of the kind of theology we have been developing here. In other words, these four marks or signs of the church need to be filtered through the lens of the Trinitarian, eschatological pneumatology we have been exploring. God's mission to the world is to draw it back into the realm of his own love, to bring it to new creation. These four marks of the church need to be viewed as an answer to this fundamental question: what kind of community is needed to engage in the mission of God to the world. Answer? It needs to be one, it needs to be holy, it needs to be catholic and it needs to be apostolic.

The Church is One

Put simply, if the church is to engage in the mission of God to the world, it needs to be united. And if it is to be united, it needs the Holy Spirit, who alone brings unity. The unity of the church is not something to be yearned for, much less a human creation, it is the gift of the Spirit: 'For we were all baptised by one Spirit into one body – whether Jews or Greeks, slave or free – and we were all given the one Spirit to drink' (1 Cor. 12.13).

Chapter 4 looked in some detail at the book of Ephesians from the perspective of what it has to say about the purpose of the world and human character. It also presents perhaps the most profound and wide-ranging ecclesiology in the New Testament.[1] If the purpose of God is to 'bring all things in

---

1. For a development of some of the theology of Ephesians and its relationship to mission, see Chapter 10 of Tomlin, G., *The Provocative Church* (London: SPCK, 2008).

heaven and earth together under one head, even Christ', and the church is the community that provides a foretaste of the new humanity, and the eschatological promise of the coherence of all things in Christ, then the unity of the church becomes a pivotal part of its witness.

A divided and fragmented church will always bear at best a muted witness to the God whose intention is to bring all things together under Christ. If God cannot do it in his own household, how can he do it to the whole of creation? Here again in Ephesians, the same order is visible – the unity of the church is important not just so that Christian people can get on well, and to make it nicer in church than outside, but because unity is vital to the mission of the church. It is precisely because the church is the community of the kingdom, those called out to bear witness to the day when God will bring all things together under Christ, that it needs to be united, it needs to be one.

Unity is not something we create, but something we receive. The Spirit is the one who creates unity – we simply are charged with the task of preserving and maintaining it. Paul makes the point in Ephesians that only a united church can bear witness to God's plan for all creation (or at least all that wants to) to be brought together under Christ. He then goes on to show how this unity can be maintained: 'Make every effort to keep the unity of the Spirit through the bond of peace. There is one body and one Spirit – just as you were called to one hope when you were called – one Lord, one faith, one baptism; one God and Father of all, who is over all and through all and in all' (Eph. 4.3–5).

The principle of unity in the Christian church can never be a particular liturgical form, because differences of culture, personality, preference and epoch mean that styles and forms of worship will always differ. The catholic creeds provide a form of unity around which the church gathers, yet it is hard to go beyond those to find agreement across the whole Christian church in any more precise doctrinal statement. In any case, creeds cannot in themselves give the dynamic unity the church needs to engage in this mission. They give a sense of identity, but do not animate the church into a radical engagement with its purpose. The true principle of unity for the church in the New Testament is the Holy Spirit. It is precisely the 'unity of the Spirit' that is to be preserved.

It is possible to experience the presence of God in the Spirit in a wide variety of forms of worship, or expressions of church life. With a keen expectation of the Spirit's presence, an openness to meet the Spirit who moves where he wills, working through us but free from our control, a sense of unity can be found in the presence of the one Spirit, beyond the different interpretations of Christian theology or liturgical form. The Holy's Spirit's characteristic work is to bring unity out of diversity and difference. As Paul puts it in 1 Corinthians 12: 'There are different kinds of gifts, but the same Spirit. There are different kinds of service, but the same Lord. There are different kinds of working, but the same God works all of them in all men. Now to each one the manifestation of the Spirit is given for the common good.'

Maintaining the unity of the Spirit might mean several things. For one, it means refraining from the depressingly universal habit of Christian tribalism, leading to public criticism of other Christian churches. Instead, as far as possible, it means speaking well of all other Christians, to value their contribution to the whole. Whether it is one denomination critical of another, evangelicals criticising catholics, or liberals criticising evangelicals, mutual suspicion is sadly endemic in many Christian churches and circles. I remember a church I once attended where from the front there were frequent small digs at other Christians whose theology was not as correct or who worshipped differently from us. Nothing huge, just regular sniping from the trenches at other Christians who had not got it quite as right as we had. This church also experienced a fair amount of internal tension, differing agendas and not much unity of purpose or vision. It was not until much later that I made the connection between the two. Public criticism of other

Christians gives permission for everyone else in the church to criticise each other, including the leadership of the church itself! An atmosphere of criticism breeds criticism. A sense of spiritual superiority towards others breeds the same thing within that church.

Such sniping also has a disastrous evangelistic effect. Any critical unbelieving visitor to a church where criticism of other Christians is regular and rife, is likely to leave very thankful that these Christians no longer have the power to fight each other in the way they did in the past in the religious wars or cultural crusades. Such a condemnatory spirit only confirms a secular society's worst fears – that Christians, given half a chance, would end up killing each other again over religious differences. Religion is shown up again as an obvious source of division and violence rather than peace and harmony, and so must be restrained as much as possible from having any impact on wider society. Public division is missiologically suicidal.[2]

Another element is a clear sense of vision. When the Spirit comes, new identity and purpose emerge, purpose that leads to a much clearer sense of direction and vision. Vision breeds unity, because then people know where the church is going, and if they don't want to go there, the bottom line is they don't have to: there are many other communities to join with different purposes. A lack of vision breeds disunity, because all kinds of competing agendas jostle for prominence, and leadership becomes a matter of keeping the peace between rival versions of the church's future. Churches are like bicycles. The moment you stop moving you fall off. Unity is fostered by vision. A clearly owned sense of vision that is big enough to excite loyalty and concrete enough to be viable is a crucial element of preserving the unity of the church that is the gift of God. Vision preserves the unity of the Spirit because church members can have a sense that they are all working towards a similar goal, whatever part of the church they happen to be involved in. A church that is in step with the Spirit will find a sense of urgency springing up,

---

2. It is interesting to note that many 'emerging church' circles display a marked desire to get beyond Christian tribalism. See Gibbs, E. and Bolger, R., *Emerging Churches: Creating Christian Community in Postmodern Culture* (London, SPCK, 2006), 34–39.

to be involved in God's work to reconcile the world to himself in Christ and to be involved in the transformation of the world. It will have direction and momentum around which a kind of dynamic unity can be found, rather than the static unity of agreement on doctrinal statements or liturgical style.

The Church is Holy

If the book of Ephesians can again serve as a guide to our ecclesiology, the church is chosen in Christ before all ages with the purpose of it being a holy people (1.4). It grows together to become a holy temple, fit to be the dwelling place of God on earth (2.21). Christ gave himself up to make a holy people for God 'radiant … without stain or wrinkle or any other blemish' (5.26f). Holiness stands right at the heart of divine desire for the church. Holiness is the sign of the presence of the *Holy* Spirit.

Ephesians suggests that all of salvation history, stretching from a divine decree before the beginning of time, through to the death of Christ on the cross, has as its purpose the creation of a people who reflect his own glory and holiness. The destiny of creation is to be formed into Christ-like shape, as Christ is the exact image of God in physical form. As Clark Pinnock puts it: 'the purpose of cosmogenesis is Christogenesis: the goal of creation is new creation in Christ.[3]

The church is meant to be the showcase of this new humanity: 'His intent was that now, through the church, the manifold wisdom of God should be made known to the rulers and authorities in the heavenly realms …' The church is the exhibition where God displays his wisdom, a prototype of his new humanity. As we have seen, this presumes the unity of the church to demonstrate the overcoming of ancient ethnic and cultural division. It also presumes the holiness of church, to demonstrate the overcoming of the destructive behaviour that led to the disintegration of humanity and of the whole creation.

In other words, for the church to engage in the mission of

---

3. Pinnock, C., *Flame of Love: A Theology of the Holy Spirit*, 74.

God, it needs to embody what it is talking about. If the church is a sign of the new creation, a foretaste of what the kingdom of God is like, it needs to be in significant ways distinct and different from other communities. In other words it needs to be holy. It needs to be a place where holiness of life, relationships and the use of resources are found, nurtured and learnt.

Throughout the history of the church, a long debate has taken place over the origin of the holiness of the church. It took classic form in the argument between St Augustine of Hippo and the North African Donatist movement in the fourth and fifth centuries. The Donatists essentially argued that the holiness of the church derives fundamentally from the holiness of its members. The church is holy only insofar as its members are holy. Therefore Donatist churches were quite rigorous places, with strict demands of membership and the purity of the lives of its ministers and priests.

The Augustinian view was that the holiness of the church derives not from its members but from Christ. The church is holy because it is the bride of Christ, however holy or unholy its members happen to be at any particular time. Just as a wife is still a wife to her husband however unfaithful she may be, or a son is still a son however he may run away, live a life of crime and end up in prison, so the church is still the holy people of God regardless of the relative holiness of the people who make up the church at any one time.

These two approaches have been replayed time and time again in the history of the church, not least at the time of the Reformation, in the disputes between the Augustinian view of those such as Luther and Calvin and the more radical wing of leaders like Andreas Karlstadt or Menno Simons.

Both views have their strengths and weaknesses. The Augustinian view preserves the vital link between Christ and the church. It allows for the inevitable presence of sin in the church, and retains a sense that the church's future and fortunes are ultimately in the hands of Christ not us, which is something of a relief! At the same time, it can allow a sense of complacency to creep in, that it doesn't really matter too much whether the actual people in the church are living holy, distinct and Christ-like lives, because it is all down to Christ in the end.

The Donatist view has a sense of urgency for holiness. It retains strong incentives for church people to live distinctive, good lives, emphasising their difference from the society around them and their being called out of that society to serve the purposes of the kingdom. However, such communities can be very hard on Christian failure and sin. They can forget that churches are gatherings of the weak, frail and sinful, not the pure and complete – they are hospitals as well as armies. They can be very moralistic in their message and condemning of those who fail.

So who is right? Well, as often is the case in such disputes, there is an element of truth and value in both, yet perhaps the order and relationship between these two insights into the nature and role of the church is the vital thing here. The church is first and foremost holy because it belongs to Christ. Its holiness does not derive from itself, but from its relation to God in Christ. Christians are holy not because they have achieved a standard of superior holiness to others through discipline and devotion, but because they belong to Christ. However, this is not the end of the story. God's gift of holiness enables holiness to grow as an embedded quality within Christian people. The realisation and experience of forgiveness, cleansing, renewal in Christ becomes a motivation and an impetus to develop holiness of character. Being part of a community where holiness is seen, experienced and lives provides a set of models to enable us to learn what holiness looks like and to imitate it. The holiness that comes from Christ comes first, and the holiness of Christians follows. As 1 Peter puts it: 'But just as he who called you is holy, so be holy in all you do; for it is written: "Be holy, because I am holy"' (1 Pet. 1.15f). Holiness therefore derives its character and shape from God.

Without the holiness of Christ, the call for personal or corporate holiness becomes anxious, strenuous, legalistic, and leads to a subtle form of spiritual pride ('look how holy I have become!'). With the holiness of Christ, practical holy goodness of character becomes possible, and in such a way that avoids destructive pride, because it leaves no sense that such character is self-taught or achieved.

Church therefore becomes a place where the qualities of life in the kingdom of God can be learnt and can grow. It is to be a place of personal and corporate transformation, to enable people to play their part in the mission of God to the world. We are talking here about sanctification, and of course the Holy Spirit is the one who makes holy.

St Basil, in his great and hugely influential work *On the Holy Spirit*, describes the Spirit as being like a place in which we are made holy. He argues that the only way we can be made holy, in other words, to be made like God, is to be in the Spirit.[4] He is the Spirit of Holiness – the one who makes holy and who produces holiness. In particular, this means the Spirit's work in making Christ-like people. If the Spirit's work is to unite us with Christ so that we share his relationship with both the Father and with the world, this means a gradual process of spiritual formation and conformity to the pattern of the life of Christ. In one sense, the Spirit's work can be described as instantaneous: it can be a sudden experience to know the deep love of the Father, or to begin to feel compassion for the pain of the world. Paul expresses this idea thus: 'I want to know Christ, and the power of his resurrection, and the fellowship of his sufferings, becoming like him in his death, and so somehow to attain to the resurrection from the dead' (Phil. 3.10). Yet this also conveys the sense that being united with Christ also presupposes and initiates a process of conformity to Christ, so that knowing this new identity and vocation become habitual, regular, part of the fabric of daily life, as it was for Jesus himself. As Clark Pinnock puts it: 'by the Spirit we enter into union with Christ and begin the journey towards transformation.'[5]

Holiness is Christ-like character. It means steady, focused

---

4. St Basil, *On the Holy Spirit* (Crestwood, New York: St Vladimir's Press, 1980), Ch. 62, 94.
5. Pinnock, *Flame of Love*.

attention, not just to bringing people to faith, or engaging them in programmes of active service in communities, but also on the Spirit's slow and sure work of building holiness in the lives of those who are set on the path of walking with Christ in the Spirit. There are many means through which holiness grows, two major ones being the practice of spiritual disciplines and regular engagement with worship.

Spiritual Disciplines

I have written elsewhere of the way in which churches can act like gyms – communities in which, through steady application to regular practices and exercises, a quality of life can develop that enables people to do things they would otherwise be unable to do.[6] Just as in gyms, a commitment to regular exercise can build physical health and fitness that enables you to play tennis, run up stairs, bend over without cricking your back and live longer. In a similar way, regular spiritual disciplines can build the quality of what we might call 'spiritual fitness' – the ability to keep your promises, remain faithful to your spouse, be generous even when short of cash, tell the truth and retain a proper humility even when everyone tells you that you are wonderful!

Practising the spiritual disciplines is by no means an alternative to trusting in the Holy Spirit as the author of holiness. As we have seen, the Spirit works largely through human action and process, while retaining a freedom from human control. Spiritual disciplines are not to be thought of as some kind of automatic route to spiritual maturity. Spiritual disciplines do not make us holy: the Holy Spirit does. The disciplines cultivate the attitude of the mind and heart in which the Spirit can do his work. They bring us into the place where the Spirit makes us holy, as Basil would have said. For example, the practice of silence tears us away from the distraction of having always to speak, thinking of what to say next, leaving a silence in which we can hear God speaking to us, and in which

6. Tomlin, G., *Spiritual Fitness: Christian Character in a Consumer Culture* (London: Continuum, 2006).

we can pay attention to his work in our hearts and in the world. The discipline of study, particularly regular study of the Bible, teaches us God's habitual way of speaking and acting – his tone of voice, so to speak. It therefore forms our minds so that they become capable of recognising the presence and work of the Spirit in the world. The point of Bible study is not just to become an expert on the Bible for its own sake, but so that we might discern what God is doing and what he is not doing in the life of his world, as he works through the Spirit to bring creation to its fulfilment.

One of the chief spiritual disciplines that builds holiness is worship. One of the essential patristic insights about Christian worship is that it has the potential to transform those who engage in it. St Paul hints at this in 2 Corinthians 3.18: 'And we, who with unveiled faces all behold the Lord's glory, are being transformed into his likeness with ever-increasing glory, which comes from the Lord, who is the Spirit.' In the fourth century, Gregory of Nyssa's theology of holiness took this further. For him, human nature can only reach its full potential in contemplation of the divine and this happens in worship: 'human nature … cannot become beautiful until it draws near to the Beautiful, and becomes transformed by the image of the divine beauty.'[7] Worship is a kind of beholding – holding something before your gaze and fixing attention on it for a sustained period of time, so that you become like the thing you look on.

Now such sustained attention is difficult in a noisy culture full of distraction. It is also made more difficult if the forms in which worship presents itself are themselves unfamiliar and alien to a generation not brought up on organ or choral music, or corporate liturgical versicles and responses. If the heart of worship is a sustained engagement with God, a steady paying attention to the grace, mercy, holiness and love of God in Christ, then this needs to be enabled in whatever cultural form or clothing is accessible in different societies. Worship is the regular resolve to remove ourselves from the focus of

7. Musurillo, H. (ed.), *From Glory to Glory: Texts from Gregory of Nyssa's Mystical Writings* (Crestwood, New York: St Vladimir's Seminary Press, 2001), 186.

our attention, and instead to place God at the centre of that attention, both individually and corporately. It needs to be both culturally attuned to minimise distraction, yet counter-cultural in that it enables encounter with the otherness and mystery of God. This might be through choral music, chamber choirs or organs; it might equally be through a worship band and contemporary 'soft rock'; it might be through Hip Hop or R&B music. The key criteria are firstly whether it enables the kind of contemplation Gregory talks about, and secondly whether it presents in a form that minimises unnecessary cultural dissonance between the cultural preferences of potential worshippers, and the practice of worship itself. Such attention also takes time and even repetition, either in the recurrent songs of more charismatic styles of worship, the formulaic quality of liturgical structure or the repeated sung phrases of Taizé worship. Whatever the style, fixing the 'eyes of the heart' on God takes time and sustained attention. A distracted mind, coming to church from all kinds of anxieties and concerns, needs longer than a quick hymn to fix attention where it needs to be: on the face of God in Christ.

A further spiritual discipline is what many churches call Prayer Ministry, offering oneself to be prayed for, as the Holy Spirit is invited to come to minister to those who ask for his presence and help. It is a way of practising regular invocation of the Holy Spirit upon the congregation which, as we have seen, is vital for a community that does not own the Spirit, but needs constantly to ask for him. People who are called to be part of God's mission in the world will find the focus of their activity not so much in the church itself, but in the world: in the housing estates, the workplace, in families, pubs and clubs, the places where the Christian life is lived and breathed. Involvement in the ordinariness of life while retaining a sense of the new vocation to God's mission in the world is hard work. It needs constant refreshing, energising and gradual growth in holiness. Every church community needs some kind of similar ministry regularly because every Christian and each Christian community needs the opportunity to be prepared, refreshed and formed for this mission in the world. If such prayer ministry becomes merely feel-good religion, simply therapy for hurting souls, then it has lost its purpose. It is a mistake to see prayer ministry in primarily therapeutic terms. Its true purpose is a form of equipping for mission – the healing of bruised souls so that they can truly and freely play their part in the church's task of bearing witness to the kingdom of God.

The path of exercising the spiritual disciplines can seem a lonely one, conjuring up images of the solitary hermit in his cell, doing battle with the demons through an iron spiritual constitution. If Christ-like holiness of character is to be developed that is capable of bearing witness to the nature and holiness of God, then small communities of mutual support, learning and nurture will be vital. These can become places where mission is resourced through a combination of the exploration of ideas and Christian teaching ('head'), identity formed through community ('heart') and pursued in the contexts of family life, location and vocation '(home').[8]

Most growing churches have such communities. They meet in homes, sometimes hosted by families, in which learning, worship and mission actively take place. They are integral to facilitating a way of living in the Spirit, both enabling the growth of personal virtue and wisdom, giving space for the development of spiritual gifts, and building a community within which relationships can develop and mission take place. These can become the basic unit of church life, and will often engage corporately in the practical activity of the kingdom – painting an elderly person's house, clearing a garden or volunteering at a homeless centre.

These are communities where the standards are kept high and where it becomes just a little easier to lead a life of holiness. An example of the dynamic of the relationship between community life, holiness and mission is found in the instruction in Ephesians 5.3–4: 'But among you there must not be even

8. MacLaren, D., *Mission Implausible: Restoring Credibility to the Church* (Milton Keynes: Paternoster, 2004).

a hint of sexual immorality, or of any kind of impurity, or of greed, because these are improper for God's holy people. Nor should there be obscenity, foolish talk or coarse joking, which are out of place, but rather thanksgiving.' To modern ears this all sounds prudish and moralistic. However, the point – in a world that is obsessed with sex and greed – is to create a space where it becomes possible to live a life that is less dominated by them. A community where these things are not the constant topic of conversation, where jokes, hopes and desires are not always around sexual conquest or getting rich, is a place where we learn a different way of life, a different set of values. The church is not to focus on these things not because sex or money are bad, but because an excessive absorption with money or sex becomes destructive of people, communities and environments, leading to lust and greed, not love and generosity. Such communities can become seedbeds of holiness, enabling Christians to live lives of purity and holiness, which in turn reflect the holiness of God, and thus spreading the aroma of Christ in the world (2 Cor. 2.15). These groups therefore need to retain a missional focus: they enable holiness of life, learnt together, which is vital for the mission of the church. A church that lives a thinly-veiled religious version of secular life, where it is hard to tell the difference between Christian life and any other style of life will be blunt and ineffective when it comes to evangelism and mission. Why get involved in something that offers nothing distinctive or different? When we do encounter it, however, holiness is provocative: it provokes a reaction, which can be sometimes positive, sometimes negative. It provokes thought, wonder and questions, questions that lead to effective evangelism and mission.

The Church is Catholic

If the heart of faith is seen as a particular doctrine, considered as the absolute core of the faith, then that doctrine must be defended and preserved at all costs. Theological exploration and discussion becomes a matter of working out how to protect and guard that doctrine. If on the other hand, Christian faith is at its heart an encounter with God in Christ through the Spirit, then that gives a more relaxed posture of exploration, an openness to learn from others, and the possibility of recognising the presence of the Spirit in many different places in the catholic or worldwide church.

A commitment to the catholicity of the church deliberately veers away from partisanship and sectarianism. It doesn't mean a denial of particular characteristics and resemblances that any particular church or tradition might have, but it does mean that the sense of being part of the whole Christian church across the world and the ages is stronger than the sense of being separate from other churches by virtue of theological or spiritual distinctiveness. This is what Cyril of Jerusalem was getting at in his famous advice: 'And if ever you are staying in a city, inquire not simply where the Lord's house is – for the sects of the profane also attempt to call their own dens, houses of the Lord – nor merely where the church is, but where is the *catholic* Church. For this is the peculiar name of the holy body, the mother of us all.'[9] The one thing that reassures us we are in a true *Christian* church is this sense of catholicity – being linked to all churches everywhere that hold to the apostolic faith (for more of which see the next section!)

In healthy churches, there is an awareness of distinct identity, a sense of location, an acknowledgement of the people and influences that have shaped and helped produce its current form, yet at the same time a reluctance to be defined by those things, because they can erode this sense of the true catholicity of the church. Labels, whether of denomination or spirituality, have value as descriptors, yet very often they can unconsciously or subconsciously serve to divide one group from another, or even foster a sense of spiritual superiority over other Christians.

Moreover, a theology of the Spirit who brings unity can help us to view doctrinal and spiritual diversity within apostolic

---

9. Cyril of Jerusalem, *Catechetical Lectures*, XVIII.26.

limits in a different context from the history of division and
schism. One way of reading the history of the church is to
see it as a series of arguments over theology and practice,
leading to ever-increasing fragmentation over the centuries
into denominational atomisation. This reading needs to be
taken seriously, highlighting the scandal of division and the
failure of the church to find unity in its desire to articulate
the truth. Another, more missional reading of the same story
describes it as the process whereby, in reaction to new cultures
and challenges, the church has discovered new resources in its
own life and belief to meet those challenges, the sum total of
which is a growing awareness of the richness of the catholic
faith. In this reading, different denominations preserve different
aspects of the catholic faith, most or perhaps even all of which
are needed at particular times of its life and mission. So for
example, at the risk of over-simplifying hugely, the Roman
Catholic Church preserves the importance of the visible unity
of the church as the presence of Christ on earth, an extension
of the incarnation, and as a place for growth in holiness. The
Orthodox remind the rest of the church of the essential mystery
of God and salvation as a restoration of the divine image in
humanity. The Lutherans remind us that we are brought into a
right relationship with God not by our own efforts, but by the
grace of God, received by simple trust. The Anglicans serve
as a reminder of the need for patient theological enquiry, the
importance of holding different Christians together under the
umbrella of a generous Christian orthodoxy, particularly in
catholic and reformed traditions. Baptists stress the importance
of the local church as an expression of the life of Christ and
the need for a conscious adult faith, not just a second-hand
one derived from parents. The Pentecostals are a reminder of
the need for the dynamic presence and experience of God in
the Spirit, and a vibrancy and expectation in worship. Each of
them in different ways preserves something of the richness of
the catholic faith, and each in a sense needs the others. This
is not to say that division into denominations is necessarily a

good thing. In fact it is to argue that each church needs to retain its identity and be true to the gift God has given it, its distinct contribution to the whole catholic church. Neither is it to say there is no room for genuine theological debate and sometimes even honest disagreement over the relevant emphasis to be placed on these factors. Yet in the broadest sense, overriding all this is a conviction that we each need one another to bear adequate witness to the 'manifold wisdom of God' (Eph. 3.10).

This ecumenical catholicity is an outcome of the presence of and emphasis on the work of the Holy Spirit. If the Holy Spirit is the 'Spirit of unity' (Rom. 5.5; Eph. 4.3), the effect of the presence of the Spirit will be to emphasise the essential unity of the church's life and theology. The Spirit brings about a consciousness of what unites Christians rather than what divides us, and a sense that what unites us is far greater and stronger than what divides us. This will even be true of the church's theology! To focus on the Holy Spirit by developing a separate, polemical 'charismatic' theology that offers a distinct and superior form of theology than others, is to miss the point. The coming of the Spirit does not create new theologies that improve on or refute others. Instead it brings alive the best of all Christian theology – Catholic, Protestant, Orthodox, Pentecostal and the rest.

At a conference on evangelism once, I fell into conversation with a Roman Catholic priest, where we began to discuss the sense of unity experienced on the conference. As we spoke of the size of the task facing the church, the calling to bear witness to the coming kingdom of God, he gave voice to the vital missional dimension of catholicity: 'This mission is just too big for any one of us. We need each other.' Here was a sense of the need for the whole catholic church, not just a part of it, to do justice to the task of involvement in the *missio dei* to the world. In order to engage in its mission the church desperately needs a sense of catholicity, which is the gift of the Holy Spirit.

The Church is Apostolic

The word 'mission' hardly appears in the New Testament. It comes of course from the Latin word *mittere*, to send, and the Greek word for someone who is sent is *apostolos*. Now this word does appear quite often in the New Testament. The idea of being 'sent' is everywhere. Christ is sent into the world by the Father (Jn. 5.37). The Father sends the Spirit (Jn. 14.26). This is precisely the prodigal Spirit we have been considering: the Spirit who goes out into the world in a kind of lavish generosity of heart, longing to lead creation back into the love between the Father and the Son, following the pathway blazed by Jesus, the incarnate Son of God. In other words, apostolicity begins with the sending of the Son and Spirit by the Father.

The disciples are sent into the world *in the same way* as Jesus is sent into the world (Jn. 17.18; 20.21). This new community of the Spirit is called by the Father to continue the work of the Son in the world. The church is sent into the world just as Christ was sent into the world by the Father, empowered by the Spirit. The apostolic nature of the church comes from its relationship to Jesus – as the people of Jesus, sent into the world to do what Jesus did: to preach, to heal, to pray, to subdue the forces of evil, to suffer, endure and eventually to triumph, all in the power of the Spirit.

This is why prayer for healing, addressing global poverty, evangelism, and engaging with issues such as depression, marital breakdown and problems of debt are a vital part of the church's ministry – because it is sent into the world to do what Jesus did in the power of the Spirit. These were precisely the things that Jesus did – healing the sick, feeding the hungry, inviting people back into fellowship with God, healing broken relationships and forgiving sins.

One of the crucial ways for a church to retain this sense of apostolicity is through the telling of and listening to stories, especially of those who have recently come to faith, or who are seeking it. A church that encourages the telling of stories is one that celebrates growth, movement, discovery of the ongoing work of God through the Spirit. These might be stories of renewed faith, faith found for the first time, or of physical healing. A church that just listens to the voice of the clergy or its own members will soon turn inward, and lose its sense of being sent into the world. A church that listens closely to the voices of those outside the church, or those on their way in (or even on their way out!), will keep the church aware of its place in the world as sent by God to be a blessing to the world, learning in what precise way it can be a blessing.

These stories serve as a constant reminder of the calling of the church to be where God is, always on the move, never satisfied and complacent, always engaged in the transformation of individuals and society. Hearing such stories constantly reminds the church of its true identity – a community sent into the world to bring about change. A church that does not constantly remind itself that God is constantly in action, a 'fast' God, always moving and beckoning the church to be involved in his work in the transformation of the world, may quickly lose its urgency, and may quickly develop a sense of being withdrawn from the world rather than sent into it.

The Spirit fills people and churches for a purpose. It is not that life may become more successful or problems solved. It is so that those people might be sent back with hope and purpose into the workplace, the family, the school to play their God-given role as agents of the kingdom of heaven. The apostolicity of the church is a reminder that the church does not exist for itself, but it exists to serve the mission of God in the world. This means that the church can never see itself as a club for those who happen to like religion. As soon as it does this, and begins to focus itself on its own life and organisation, it begins to lose its way. This is the constant temptation of the church – to become so interested in its own internal agenda, tidying its own house and getting its theology or liturgy right, that it loses the will to invite others to know Christ, it forgets that it is sent into the world to set up signs of the new creation that will one day come. Churches can always think of good reasons to avoid the challenges of mission and evangelism. It is always an easier life to settle for church management and maintenance. Keeping evangelism, the act and posture of hospitality at the very core of the church's life, keeps it open, welcoming, and responsive to the world.

The apostolicity of the church is a reminder that the reason it strives to be one, holy and catholic is that it can play its proper role in the world – sent just as Jesus was, to remind a broken and damaged world that it is the wonderful creation of a God of love, and that only by returning to that love, can it find the healing, maturity and fulfilment that it craves. Being apostolic means being sent, but not sent alone. It means being co-opted, enlisted, engaged by the prodigal Spirit, who invites us to join him in a life of intimacy with the Father and the Son, and the privilege of seeing creation renewed, as the Spirit works in the world.

The church has always counted its birthday as the day of Pentecost. The church came into existence not at Christmas, nor on Good Friday, nor even on Easter Day, but on the day when the Spirit came. The Holy Spirit and the church are inextricably linked, so much so that without the Spirit, the church does not really exist. The Spirit constitutes the church, because it is only by the Spirit that people are drawn into relationship with the Father through being united with Jesus the Son, and therefore into relationships with each other. A church that does not constantly pray the prayer 'Come Holy Spirit', expecting an answer to that prayer, will not only lack energy and vision, it will also lose its own identity and purpose. A church that does constantly pray that prayer expectantly, will seldom be a dull place, and will always have that freshness that comes from the Spirit who makes all things new.

CONCLUSION

Michael Welker writes: 'Love in the power of the Spirit is the power of God's self-demonstration, the power by which God rules the world.'[1] That sums up much of what this book has been trying to say. The work of the Spirit is to bring creation to its fulfilment and its true destiny in the love of God. And he does that by drawing people into Christ, giving them new identity and purpose, so that they can be conformed to him, capable of God-like love in human form, love that is prepared to go to a cross for the sake of the beloved. The Spirit comes from love, draws us back into love, teaches love and ultimately enfolds all things in love, because this is precisely 'the power by which God rules the world'.

Life in the Spirit is thus both radically inclusive and radically exclusive. The Spirit reaches out to all of life and all of creation in the love of God. Once we are in the Spirit, nothing that is created can be foreign to us, because all God created is good and capable of redemption. The Spirit touches all of life and is there for all people. At the same time this is no generalised Hegelian 'world-Spirit', it is the Spirit of Christ alone, the Spirit who draws us into the love of the Father for the Son. This is the prodigal Spirit, who goes out from the Father to draw the world, and us, back into Christ. The Spirit alone brings life. And true life is found in Christ. If we are to be fully alive, capable of the love for which we were made, we need the Spirit.

Maintaining openness to the Holy Spirit is therefore vital

---

1. Welker, M., *God the Spirit* (Minneapolis: Fortress, 1994).

if we are to be opened up to this love that beats at the heart of all things. Yet it can be unsettling because in the realm of the Spirit, we are not in control. It was 'in the Spirit' that John began to have all kinds of unsettling revelations of what was really going on in the present and the future as the Roman empire and apathy threatened the fledgling churches in Asia (Rev. 1.10). It is easier to write about the Spirit than genuinely to open myself to his gentle (and sometimes not so gentle) workings. We are very good at finding ways of keeping control in our religious activity, either through tightly choreographed liturgy, closely argued theology or carefully prepared sermons (not that there is anything wrong with good liturgy, precise theology or thorough sermons!). They have somehow, however, to leave room for the Spirit who blows where he wills. It is not in the church only that this needs to happen. If the Spirit is truly and constantly working to bring all creation to its fulfilment, then that posture of openness to the surprising Spirit of God is vital not just during worship but also when browsing the internet, on the beach, eating a meal with friends, walking the dog, talking to neighbours or reading a novel. Gaining a better understanding of the theology of the Spirit is not enough: we need to learn life in the Spirit. This book ends then with a question: how might you (and I – I include myself in this) maintain this posture of openness to the Spirit who is looking to draw us into the love of the Father in Christ today? And tomorrow? How might this become a way of life for us? How might we explore our Spirit-taught new identity as beloved children of God and our new purpose as called to be involved in God's work to reconcile all things under Christ today?

Christian faith was never meant to be a system of following carefully prescribed laws or instructions. Instead it is praying in the Spirit (Eph. 6.18), worship in the Spirit (Phil. 3.3), discerning the Spirit (1 Cor. 2.15). It is none other than life in the Spirit (1 Pet. 4.6). If Christian people can learn to live this way more and more, finding realistic, visible and sustainable ways to express that life and the love of the Father for the Son in the Spirit in these globalised, interconnected yet still struggling societies, then there will be hope not just for us, but for our churches, our communities and our world.

BIBLIOGRAPHY

Abraham, W. J., *The Logic of Evangelism*, London: Hodder, 1989.

Aristotle, *The Nicomachean Ethics*, Penguin Classics, H. Tredennick, London: Penguin, 1953.

Augustine, 'On the Spirit and the Letter', *Saint Augustine's Anti-Pelagian Works*, B. B. Warfield, Edinburgh: T&T Clark, 1991.

Badcock, G. D., *Light of Truth and Fire of Love: A Theology of the Holy Spirit*, Grand Rapids: Eerdmans, 1997.

Barth, K., *Dogmatics in Outline*, London: SCM, 1985.

Barth, K. and D. Ritschl, *The Theology of Schleiermacher: Lectures at Göttingen, winter semester of 1923/24*, Edinburgh: T&T Clark, 1982.

Basil, S., *On the Holy Spirit*, Crestwood, New York: St Vladimir's Seminary Press, 1980.

Baucum, T., *Evangelical Hospitality: Catechetical Evangelism in the Early Church and its Recovery for Today*, Lanham, ML: Scarecrow Press, 2008.

Blomberg, C. L., *Contagious Holiness: Jesus' Meals with Sinners*, Downers Grove: IVP, 2005.

Bosch, D. J., *Transforming Mission: Paradigm Shifts in Theology of Mission*, Maryknoll, New York: Orbis Books, 1991.

Bretherton, L., *Hospitality as Holiness: Christian Witness amid Moral Diversity*, Aldershot: Ashgate, 2006.

Bretherton, L., *Christianity and Contemporary Politics: The Conditions and Possibilities of Faithful Witness*, Chichester: Wiley-Blackwell, 2010.

Burgess, S. M., *The Holy Spirit: Medieval Roman Catholic and Reformation Traditions*, Peabody, MA: Hendricksen, 1997.

Calvin, J., *Institutes of the Christian Religion*, London: Collins, 1975, 1986.

Cantalamessa, R., *Come, Creator Spirit*, Collegeville, Minnesota: Liturgical Press, 2003.

Cartledge, M. J., *Encountering the Spirit: The Charismatic Tradition*, London: Darton, Longman & Todd, 2006.

Dabney, D. L., 'Naming the Spirit: Towards a Pneumatology of the Cross',

Starting with the Spirit, G. Preece and S. Pickard, Hindmarsh: Australian Theological Forum, 28–59, 2001.

Dujarier, M., *A History of the Catechumenate: The First Six Centuries*, New York: Sadlier, 1979.

Edwards, J., *The Religious Affections*, Edinburgh: Banner of Truth, 1986.

Ellington, S. A., 'The Face of God as His Creating Spirit', *The Spirit Renews the Face of the Earth*, Eugene, Oregon: Pickwick, 2009.

Fee, G. D., *God's Empowering Presence: The Holy Spirit in the Letters of Paul*, Peabody, MA: Hendrickson Publishers, 1994.

Fiddes, P. S., *Participating in God: A Pastoral Doctrine of the Trinity*, London: Darton, Longman & Todd, 2000.

Finney, J., *Finding Faith Today: How Does It Happen?*, Swindon: BFBS, 1992.

Gibbs, E. and R. Bolger, *Emerging Churches: Creating Christian Community in Postmodern Culture*, London: SPCK, 2006.

Grant, R. M., Ed., *The Early Church Fathers, Irenaeus of Lyons*, London: Routledge, 1997.

Green, J. B. and M. Turner, *Jesus of Nazareth: Lord and Christ: Essays on the Historical Jesus and New Testament Christology*, Grand Rapids: Eerdmans; Carlisle: Paternoster, 1994.

Greig, P., *God on Mute: Engaging the Silence of Unanswered Prayer*, Eastbourne: Kingsway, 2007.

Gresham, J., 'The Social Model of the Trinity and its Critics', *Scottish Journal of Theology*, vol. 46, Cambridge: Cambridge University Press, 1993.

Gunton, C., 'The Spirit Moved over the Face of the Waters: The Holy Spirit and the Created Order', *Spirit of Truth and Power: Studies in Christian Doctrine and Experience*, D. F. Wright, Edinburgh: Rutherford House, 2007, pp. 56–72.

Hall, S. G., *Doctrine and Practice in the Early Church*, London: SPCK, 1991.

Hauerwas, S., *A Community of Character: Toward a Constructive Christian Social Ethic*, Notre Dame: University of Notre Dame Press, 1981.

Hauerwas, S., *Vision and Virtue: Essays in Christian Ethical Reflection*, Notre Dame: University of Notre Dame Press, 1981.

Hauerwas, S. and C. Pinches, *Christians Among the Virtues: Theological Conversations with Ancient and Modern Ethics*, Notre Dame: University of Notre Dame Press, 1997.

Hauerwas, S. and W. H. Willimon, *Resident Aliens: Life in the Christian Colony*, Nashville: Abingdon Press, 1989.

Heard, J., 'Re-evangelising Britain? An Ethnographic Analysis and Theological Evaluation of the Alpha Course', Department of Education and Professional Studies, School of Social Science and Public Policy, London: King's College, PhD, 2007.

Hunt, S., *Anyone for Alpha?*, London: Darton, Longman & Todd, 2001.

Hütter, R., 'Ecclesial Ethics, the Church's Vocations, and Paraclesis', *Pro Ecclesia* 2, 1993, p. 450.

Jüngel, E., *God as the Mystery of the World: On the Foundations of the Theology of the Crucified One in the Dispute between Theism and Atheism*, Edinburgh: T&T Clark, 1983.

Kilby, K., 'Perichoresis and Projection: Problems with the Social Doctrines of the Trinity', New Blackfriars: Blackwell, 2000.

Levison, J. R., *Filled with the Spirit*, Grand Rapids: Eerdmans, 2009.

Lewis, C. S., *The Great Divorce*, London: Geoffrey Bles, 1946.

Lindbeck, G., *The Nature of Doctrine*, New Haven: Yale University Press, 1946.

MacLaren, D., *Mission Implausible: Restoring Credibility to the Church*, Milton Keynes: Paternoster, 2004.

McClymond, M., *Encounters with God: An Approach to the Theology of Jonathan Edwards*, New York: OUP, 1998.

Metzler, N., 'The Trinity in Contemporary Theology: Questioning the Social Trinity', *Concordia Theological Quarterly 67 (3/4)*, 2003, pp. 270–87.

Moltmann, J., *The Church in the Power of the Spirit: A Contribution of Messianic Ecclesiology*, London: SCM Press, 1977.

Moltmann, J., *The Trinity and the Kingdom of God*, London: SCM, 1981.

Moltmann, J., *The Spirit of Life: A Universal Affirmation*, London: SCM, 1992.

Musurillo, H., Ed., *From Glory to Glory: Texts from Gregory of Nyssa's Mystical Writings*, Crestwood, New York: St Vladimir's Seminary Press, 2001.

Newbigin, L., *The Gospel in a Pluralist Society*, London: SPCK, 1989.

Palmer, G. E. H., Sherrard, P., et al., Eds., *The Philokalia: The Complete Text, compiled by St Nikodemos of the Holy Mountain and St Makarios of Corinth*, London: Faber & Faber, 1995.

Pascal, B., *Pensées*, Harmondsworth: Penguin, 1966.

Percy, M., ' "Join-the-dots" Christianity: Assessing ALPHA', Reviews in *Religion and Theology 4 (3)*, 1997, pp. 14–18.

Pieper, J., *The Four Cardinal Virtues*, Notre Dame: University of Notre Dame Press, 1990.

Pinnock, C., *Flame of Love: A Theology of the Holy Spirit*, Downers Grove: InterVarsity Press, 1996.

Plantinga, A., *Warranted Christian Belief*, New York: Oxford University Press, 2000.

Pohl, C., *Making Room: Recovering Hospitality as a Christian Tradition*, Grand Rapids: Eerdmans, 1999.

Prenter, R., *Spiritus Creator: Luther's Concept of the Holy Spirit*, Philadelphia: Fortress, 1953.

Rahner, K., *The Trinity*, London: Burns and Oates, 1970.

Richards, A., 'Eating Alpha', *The Alpha Phenomenon: Theology, Praxis and Challenges for Mission and Church Today*, A. Brookes, London: CTBI, 2007, pp. 330–39.

Rievaulx, A. of, *Spiritual Friendship*, Kalamazoo: Cistercian Publications, 1974.

Seitz, C., Ed., *Nicene Christianity: The Future for a New Ecumenism*, Grand Rapids: MI; Great Britain: Brazos Press, 2001.

Sheils, W. J., Ed., *The Church and Healing. Studies in Church History*, Oxford: published for the Ecclesiastical History Society by Basil Blackwell, 1982.

Suurmond, J. J., *Word and Spirit at Play: Towards a Charismatic Theology*, Grand Rapids: Eerdmans, 1995.

Tomlin, G., *The Provocative Church*, London: SPCK, 2002.

Tomlin, G., *Spiritual Fitness: Christian Character in a Consumer Culture*, London: Continuum, 2006.

Toynbee, P., *Towards the Holy Spirit*, London: SCM, 1973.

Tugwell, S., *Did You Receive the Spirit?*, London: Darton, Longman & Todd, 1972.

Volf, M., *Work in the Spirit: Towards a Theology of Work*, New York: Oxford University Press, 1991.

Ward, W. R., *The Protestant Evangelical Awakening*, Cambridge: Cambridge University Press, 1992.

Ware, K., *The Orthodox Way*, New York: St Vladimir's Seminary Press, 1979.

Weinandy, T., *The Father's Spirit of Sonship: Reconceiving the Trinity*, Edinburgh: T&T Clark, 1995.

Welker, M., *God the Spirit*, Minneapolis: Fortress, 1994.

Willard, D., *The Spirit of the Disciplines: Understanding How God Changes Lives*, London: Hodder & Stoughton, 1988.

Willard, D., *Renovation of the Heart: Putting on the Character of Christ*, Colorado Springs: NavPress, 2002.

Wright, N. T., *Jesus and the Victory of God*, London: SPCK, 1996.

Wright, N. T., *Surprised by Hope*, London: SPCK, 2007.

Wright, N. T., *Virtue Reborn*, London: SPCK, 2010.

Young, W. P., *The Shack*, London: Hodder, 2008.

Yong, A., *Hospitality and the Other: Pentecost, Christian Practices, and the Neighbor*, New York: Orbis; Edinburgh: Alban, 2008.

INDEX

CPSIA information can be obtained at www.ICGtesting.com
Printed in the USA
BVOW012135110213

312983BV00004B/20/P

9 781905 887002